".....When he had cast into the water, the waters were made sweet "Exodus 15:25

Remembering Sweetwater

The Mansions,

The Mills,

The People

By: William L. McDonald

With Rare Photos From: L.D. Staggs, Jr.

Bluewater Publications
Printed in The United States of America

This book is dedicated to William Albert Middleton,
My Great-Grandson

FOREWORD

The story of Sweetwater is a saga of two large ante-bellum tracts of land and the late Nineteenth and early Twentieth Century history of the industrial development of East Florence. This area of Florence was called Sweetwater because of its association with a spring and a creek that earlier man had labeled "Succotania'. According to tradition, this Indian word described an unusually sweet taste of the cool and clear water that flowed from the spring and ran through a beautiful valley below.

The Sweetwater plantation at the head of Sweetwater Creek is part of the story of Alabama as well as the history of Florence and Lauderdale County. It is listed on the National Register of Historic Places. Little is known of the other tract of land, also known as "Sweetwater', which was located at the mouth of Sweetwater Creek. Yet, its lands became the center of the industrial development of East Florence, which has long been referred to by those who worked in its factories and raised families in its hills and hollows as "Sweetwater'.

The history of East Florence is not only a study of a unique industrial development of the last century, but, more importantly, it is a story of a people who lived, worked, shopped and worshipped in an area where everything was within a convenient walking distance.

It is almost as if one were looking at the ancient clans of the Old World. These people held a family tie one with another, and a deep and abiding loyalty to their work places, churches, and the stores where they purchased their groceries and other necessities.

There seemed to be a code that transcended the entire area. These folks were independent, gentle and extremely proud. Their homes and communities were neatly arranged and well kept. Their children and their children's children have held a, kindred sense of belonging. This is evidenced at the annual gathering of those who have lived or worked in East Florence. It is called "The Sweetwater Reunion".

This book is about their history, a lovely story that needed to be told.

Table of Contents

Mansions & Antebellum Days

Sweetwater Plantation, home of the former Alabama Governor, Robert Patton (Painted by Dorothy Carter McDonald as remembered from her childhood.)

Sweetwater is listed on the National Register of Historic Places.

SWEETWATER
—1828—

Home of Major John Brahan, veteran War of 1812.
Major General, Alabama Militia, who owned
4,000 acres here. Built of bricks made on
the place, marble mantels imported from Italy,
boxwood hedge from London.
Named for spring nearby.

Federals and Confederates quartered here
at various times during the Civil War.

Home of Brahan's son-in-law, Robert M. Patton,
Governor of Alabama, 1865-1868.

ALABAMA HISTORICAL ASSOCIATION

Sweetwater Mansions —The Story of East Florence—

A number of years ago a writer listed "home" as probably the most beautiful word in the English language. Close kin to home would surely be the words "sweet water". In one of the most ancient manuscripts from the east, rivers of sweet water were described as flowing from a mythical mountain located at the center of the universe.

The early Indians of North Alabama discovered a large spring and a creek of clear; cold water located east of what would someday become the City of Florence. They named it "Succotania". This word was later translated into the white man's language as Sweet Water.

The Antebellum Plantation

This story of Sweetwater begins soon after the Treaty of 1816 when the Indians ceded the lands of Northwest Alabama. Settlers who had long coveted the Muscle Shoals were staking out their claims and bidding for their titles. John Brahan was one of these early investors.

Born in Virginia on June 6, 1774, Brahan was appointed Receiver of Public Moneys for the land office at Nashville in June 1809. To facilitate the land sales in the Alabama Territory, Brahan moved with the land office to Huntsville in 1811. He built a large brick residence at the spring that would one day supply water for the historic Merrimac Cotton Mill. This small lake of sparkling water known as Brahan Spring is the centerpiece of a lovely Twentieth Century park in Huntsville.

The Great Land Sales of 1818 pitted John Brahan against the wealthy Philadelphia and Nashville investors. This brought him into conflict with such men as John Coffee, Andrew Jackson, James Jackson, John Childress, and John Donelson of the Nashville region.

This story as it unfolds shows Brahan taking the lead in attempts by the local settlers in trying to prevent the outside investors from buying up the choicest Alabama lands. Carried away in this endeavor, Brahan purchased 44,678 acres of land valued at $318,580 using $80,000 of government money as his down payment. His role in this fight made him a local hero, of sorts, for keeping these prime tracts out of the hands of the outside land grabbers. However, a congressional committee was later called to investigate Brahan's financial matters. Although they made no specific charge against him, he was required to return the $80,000 he had spent plus 1,260 acres of land so as to satisfy the debt he owed the United States Treasury. This action by the committee in effect also cost Brahan his job. He was asked by the local trustees of the Huntsville Land Office to submit his resignation.

While in office, Brahan traveled over North Alabama at various times in keeping with his responsibilities as Receiver of Public Moneys. On one of these trips, he became acquainted with a tract of land east of Florence. On it was a large spring that served as the headwaters of a bold branch that emptied into the Tennessee River. Brahan learned that, according to legend, the Indian name for this spring and creek was Succatania, which meant Sweetwater. This tract was part of the land he purchased at the Great Land Sales of 1818.

Following a fire that destroyed his Huntsville residence Brahan decided that his new home would be at

Sweetwater. He selected a site for his manor house facing the early stage road that connected Pulaski, Tennessee, to the river port at Florence. This location was at the top of the hill above the spring.

His slaves began the excavation for the basement in 1828. Clay soil was removed to a depth of four feet under the entire area of the proposed house. This clay was made into bricks needed for the thick walls of Sweetwater using cypress molds and a primitive kiln.

The solid brick walls of the mansion had reached the height of the window sills when Brahan suddenly became sick and died. He had been on a trip to another one of his plantations located a few miles west of Como, Mississippi. He was caught in a heavy rainstorm while on his way home. By the time he reached Florence he was suffering from a severe cold. A few days later, on July 5, 1834, he died of complications from pneumonia at the home of his daughter, Jane Patton, near downtown Florence. He was buried in the woods north of the foundations of his unfinished house.

Robert M. Patton, Jane's husband, became the executor of his father-in-law's estate. The Lauderdale County plantation and the unfinished mansion were willed to the General's son, Major Robert Brahan. Robert's wife, however, strongly objected to the idea of living in the country, so the Major sold Sweetwater to Patton who swapped his town house as partial payment.

Robert Miller Patton was a politician as well as a merchant and planter. A son of William and Martha Hayes Patton, he was born in Virginia in 1809. He came with his parents to Huntsville in 1818. His father was among the founders of Bell Cotton Factory, one of the first cotton mills in the Gulf States. Robert was elected to the Alabama Legislature from Florence in 1832. He served continuously in both the House and Senate until elected Governor in 1865.

With great enthusiasm the future Governor of Alabama completed the construction of Sweetwater. He carefully followed his father-in-law's original plan. There were four large rooms divided by a central hall on the first floor. The two to the left as one entered the home were large reception rooms separated by folding doors. Originally, the dining room was the first room on the right at the main entrance. However, after the Governor's death, Jane moved the dining area to the east reception room, and used the former dining room for her bedroom. The master bedroom was the second of the two rooms on the right of the entrance hall. A small hall separated the two rooms on the right. It connected the main hallway to the carriage entrance at the south side of the house. The rooms and halls were papered with elegant designs. This feature, too, has a note of history. Their son, Billy Patton, purchased the paper in New York prior to the Civil War. A Negro slave, Sidney De Priest, carefully hanged the paper on the walls. His grandson, Oscar De Priest of Illinois, became the first Negro elected to the U. S. House of Representatives. The hardwood floors of Sweetwater were constantly rubbed and cleaned by the servants until they had an appearance of white marble.

The second floor plan followed closely the arrangement of rooms on the main floor. The southeast room was the boys' room in the earliest days. The northeast room was the guest room and the other room on that side of the house was used by the Governor's daughters.

The brick out-building near the rear of the house had three rooms: the kitchen, weaving-room, and icehouse. Ice was cut from the creek during hard winter freezes and stored in the deep well under the icehouse room. Mary, the main Negro cook, lived in the kitchen area.

The basement was the most unusual feature at Sweetwater. It is believed that no other basement of its kind exists in the historic homes of Alabama. Originally, there were five large rooms and each had its own fireplace. One of these was called the wine cellar where the best of a home-brewed vintage was made from the vineyard near the house. There were also the plantation preserving room, a great pantry, and a laundry room. There remains until this day a mystery about one of these rooms. One can see inside of it from a small window, but there are no doors to permit an entrance.

Three porches were planned for the house. The two that remain today are at the front and carriage entrances. Across the entire back part of the house, there was once a Louisiana-type porch that overlooked the trees and the walk that led down the hill to Sweetwater spring. The Pattons were probably the first in the area to install a ram. This early mechanical device was used to pump water from the spring all the way up the hill to the big house. In spite of this availability of running water, large buckets, each with a dipper, were kept on the back porch for drinking purposes.

The slave quarters were at the back of the spring on a hill above the creek. Twenty-four cabins were arranged in a square that formed a court. The largest cabin at one corner was the home of the plantation overseer. Six additional cabins were later added in a row below the square. Private gardens were laid out for each family. The square became a popular gathering place for the Negroes in the evenings after the work was done, and especially on Sunday afternoons and holidays. By 1860 there were 117 slaves living on the Sweetwater plantation.

The Pattons and their descendants made Sweetwater their home for almost 140 years. Robert Patton continued to add to and improve the plantation. Its 1,500 acres in 1850 became 3,800 acres by 1860, included land that stretched all the way to what would become the Wilson Dam Reservation on the north bank of the Tennessee River in 1918. Sweetwater Plantation also included the beautiful Patton Island in the Tennessee River where the Negroes would scoop up and crush mussel shells that were used on the main drive and walkways of the plantation.

Robert and Jane Brahan Patton had nine children. All but two of them were born at Sweetwater. Three sons were in the Confederate Army during the Civil War. Captain Billy Patton was killed at Shiloh. Sergeant Robert Patton died from wounds received near Selma in 1865. Captain Brahan Patton survived the war. He returned to Sweetwater where he remained to take care of his widowed mother following Governor Patton's death. Brahan Patton drove an elegant buggy that was pulled by his favorite mare, Dolly. Brahan would ride into town on

Saturdays. Later in the afternoon folks would see old Dolly carefully bringing her master home without the aid of her driver. It was easy, they said, for the old soldier to drown his war memories in the saloons of Florence.

There were three other sons: John, Charles and Andrew. John died young. Andrew was injured while in college and was an invalid for seven years prior to his death. Charles Hayes Patton became a prominent attorney. One of the two daughters, Marie Jane Patton, became the wife of John J. McDavid, an attorney at Huntsville. The other daughter, Martha Hayes Patton, was married to Colonel John D. Weeden after the Civil war. In her late years, Martha Patton Weeden would come home to her beloved Sweetwater during the summer months where her son, John D. Weeden, and his wife, Jessie Earthman Weeden, kept her room in waiting.

The lore of the old house would not be complete without a listing of the important personalities who were entertained there. On one visit to North Alabama, the former President of the United States, Andrew Jackson, spent the night here. During the war years, the Confederate President Jefferson Davis was a guest.

Governor Clement Clay and his wife, Virginia, were entertained, as was the great Southern orator, William L. Yancey. General William Martin and his staff made Sweetwater their headquarters for a week during the war. Another wartime Guest at the old manor house was Confederate General Gidean Pillow.

It has been written that a dwelling is a symbol of the character of its people. No other buildings or structures have so completely revealed man's culture as does the study of his home. The story of Sweetwater is far more than a tale of a vanishing architecture of ante-bellum days in the middle and deep South. It speaks softly of those who once lived among its walls.

Early Photographs

The grand front entrance to ante-bellum Sweetwater Plantation that is listed on the prestigious National Register of Historic Places in America. Standing are members of the family of Governor Robert Miller Patton (left to right): Marie Jane McDavid, Edmund McDavid, and Brahan Patton. The Governor's great-grandchildren are seated on the steps. (Photograph made about 1910.)

Alabama Governor Robert Miller Patton with wife, Jane, daughter, Mattie, and son, Bernie. Governor Patton's family occupied the Sweetwater home and plantation for almost 150 Years. The Sweetwater mansion is located at the head of Sweetwater Creek, which gave its name to the community of Sweetwater in East Florence.

A view of Sweetwater from the south showing the carriage entrance.

It was said that during the early years of the Civil War, Confederate President and Mrs. Jefferson Davis arrived at this south entrance to Sweetwater in their fine carriage which was pulled by two splendid white horses. The butler, Uncle Champ, greeted the distinguished couple and escorted them into the house where they were presented to Mr. and Mrs. Robert Miller Patton.

The kitchen at the rear of the Sweetwater manor house.

Mary, the beloved cook at Sweetwater, made her home within the walls of this kitchen along with her children. One of her sons, Sam, who brought Billy Patton's body home from the Battlefield at Shiloh, knew this kitchen as his boyhood home.

Governor Robert Miller Patton Of the Sweetwater Plantation in East Florence

The Governor was a devout Elder in the First Presbyterian Church in Florence. During the Civil War, following the arrest of his pastor by the Union Army, Governor Patton undertook the awesome responsibilities of preaching the Sunday morning sermons while his pastor was in prison.

The family of Captain John J. McDavid who was married to Marie Jane Patton, a daughter of Governor Patton. (Captain Brahan Patton, son of Governor Patton, is seated to the left on the back row.) This photograph was made about 1900 at the former Florence Synodical College (located at the present site of the Florence Post Office.)

William Patton

Father of Governor Robert M. Patton of Sweetwater. (William Patton came from Ireland and was one of the founders of the Bell Cotton Factory in Huntsville, Alabama, one of the first of the cotton industries in Alabama.) The above portrait and other Patton paintings once graced the walls of Sweetwater. Following the death of Mrs. Jesse Weeden in 1972, these portraits were donated to the Florence/Lauderdale Public library by Elizabeth Weeden Minton.

The Night Sherman's Men Raided Sweetwater

This is a story about terrorism that happened near Florence during the Civil War. It involved the family of Robert Miller Patton, who later served as governor of Alabama. The Patton home, known as Sweetwater, is located in a grove of trees alongside Florence Boulevard and is one of the area's most priceless relics of the past. The background for the story began on Nov. 3, 1863, when the 15th U.S. Army Corps moved into the small rural town of Florence. Their commander was none other than Gen. William Tecumseh Sherman, who later won lasting fame when he burned his way across Georgia. The tall, hardy and homely general made his headquarters at Wesleyan Hall on the university campus. He established his own living quarters in the spacious Gen. Samuel Weakley home that fronted both North Pine Street and North Court Street near the downtown area of the city. Florence and the surrounding countryside became an armed camp overnight. One of Sherman's divisions made encampment at Sweetwater, which in that early day was located on one of the main pikes leading into the city from the east.

The soldiers began roaming over the plantation grounds in search of spoils as soon as their tents were erected near the big spring. All the meat that had been stored for the winter was taken. Turkeys, chickens, ducks and geese were shot and tied to the saddles of raiders. All of the horses and cows was confiscated to be used in Sherman's forthcoming march to Chattanooga. The house was raided time and again. Most of the edibles, including pickles, beans, potatoes and corn, were carried away. As expected, a clean sweep of the wine cellar was made at the very beginning. Slave cabins on the grounds were used as infirmaries for soldiers suffering from smallpox. Two of the newest cabins were burned, along with the bodies of two victims as a means of preventing the further spread of the disease.

However, the night of fear that forever lived in the memories of the Pattons was different from the other raids by Sherman's men. It began about an hour before midnight and did not end until around three in the early morning on that cold November day. The two daughters, Martha and Marie Jane, were with their father and mother in the house that night. So was Marie Jane's husband, Capt. John Jackson McDavid, who was recovering from an illness, contracted while serving with the Confederate Army. All had retired for the evening when the soldiers appeared. The hero of this story was the Negro slave, Edmund Patton. Edmund, who was later to be affectionately called "Uncle Champ" by the other Negroes, must have, had a premonition that night. Rather than retiring, as was his custom after the family went to bed, Edmund waited and watched from the front steps of the mansion. It wasn't long before he heard the rattle of sabers and the sound of feet on the front driveway. On the tip of his toes, Edmund reached upward as high as he could and tapped on the window of the master bedroom. Patton quickly opened the front door. Edmund rushed in with the alarm: "Soldiers are coming!" He quickly moved toward the stairs in the main hall that led to the second floor, where the young ladies were sleeping. It was then that the invaders battered down the side door. They rushed toward the stairwell as the servant threw his arms across their path. Edmund's heroic statement made to the soldiers that night has been carefully recorded and preserved in the old plantation ledgers: "My two young mistresses are upstairs and you can not go there unless over my body."

The horrified family watched as the house was ransacked room by room. The master of the house offered a meal to the terrorists. The only food in the house was the last two turkeys, which had been baked that day. The soldiers quickly consumed both platters of meat, then drew their guns and demanded the wallets of Patton and Capt. McDavid. It was at this moment that Mrs. Patton, scared and completely exhausted, broke away and ran to her room. One of the soldiers quickly pursued her. Her screams brought the entire family to her side. They found the soldier on his knees while attempting to search her body. Mr. Patton raged at the intruder: "Touch my wife for your life!" Mrs. Patton, sensing the danger, dropped her purse, which had been concealed in her sleeve. It contained $40 in gold and greenbacks and several jewels, including three diamond studs that had belonged to her son, Capt. Billy Patton, who had died at Shiloh.

It was after 3 o'clock in the morning when the siege ended. The soldiers went away with all that they could carry. As they departed, they demanded that all the lights be extinguished. Any alarm from the family would result in their burning the house.

Sherman's stay in Florence was; brief. His memoirs say little about the area and its people. In all fairness to the general, he probably never knew about the night of violence at Sweetwater. However, the townsfolk knew and would never forget.

The Pattons remembered the heroism of old Edmund. The governor gave him a farm and built for him a comfortable house where he lived in the remaining years of his life. Miss Howard Weeden, the artist and poet, painted Uncle Champ's portrait, which was later published in one of her books. The old hero of Sweetwater was buried in the family cemetery, and a lovely marker placed over his grave by the family. However, modern-day vandals have destroyed Edmund's gravestone along with the other monuments in the ancient burying ground at Sweetwater.

Time has a way of erasing some memories. Yet, there are recollections that become engraved within the human soul as if carved in granite.

The Story of Sam at Sweetwater

Sam was one of the African-American slaves who resided on the 3,800-acre plantation east of Florence known as Sweetwater. More importantly, Sam was a Civil War hero whose name was enshrined by the gratitude of a family who never forgot his noble deed following the terrible Battle of Shiloh.

Sam went away with the Confederate Army to be with his young master, Billy Patton, the very next week following the secession of Alabama from the Union. Sam and William Anderson "Billy" Patton grew up together. Sam was born in 1837 and Billy a year later. Before the war, when Billy became a Florence merchant with his older brother, Brahan, Sam went along to drive the buggy.

Billy's father, Robert Miller Patton, who in 1865 became Governor of Alabama, owned the plantation. Sam's mother, Mary, was the family cook and lived with her children in the kitchen behind the big house.

The story of Sam at Shiloh actually had its beginning in the early Cumberland Gap Campaign in Kentucky. It was here the body of their fallen leader, General Felix Zollercoffer, was disfigured and dishonored by the Yankee soldiers. Sam resolved he would never permit this to happen to his friend, Billy.

Lieutenant William Anderson Patton, Company C, 16th Alabama Infantry, fell mortally wounded during the charge made just south of Shiloh Church on Sunday morning, April 6, 1862. This and the recovery of the body was described by his commanding officer, Captain Alexander Donelson Coffee, in his letter dated April 10, 1862:

"We here lost most of our men and here it was poor Billy fell, he was about five feet from my right ...when a ball struck him in the forehead, killing him instantly. ...I left the regiment at dust and went to look for poor Billy. I then put him in a small log hut they used for a sutler's store . . .and I walked by moonlight back to the road and camps through the ground we had fought over." However, the tide of the battle changed the following day. The 16th Alabama was in the brigade commanded by Brigadier General Sterling Alexander Martin Wood, a son of Florence's first mayor.

Wood wrote that the regiment next to his brigade on the left broke and fell back; all except two of his field officers were wounded. The entire Confederate command under

General Beauregard had no alternative but to retire to Corinth from whence they had come. The last of the staggering lines of General Breckinridge's troops filed pass the outpost of the rear guard within view of Shiloh church after 4 p.m. The Battle of Shiloh was all over except for the burying of the dead.

And thus begins the narrative that has been told and retold by generations of the Patton family. Sam refused to leave the field with the retreating Confederate Army. It was during the night when he found the sutler's hut to recover his master's body. Years later an old veteran of Green Hill remembered seeing Sam with Billy's corpse and wondered how he had made the agonizing trip from Shiloh to Corinth. But this was only the first part of the long and tedious journey that led down the Memphis Pike, across the Tennessee River, and through the front gate and the portals of the Sweetwater Plantation. Sam's homecoming was somberly described by Howard Weeden, who was connected to Sweetwater by marriage, in her poem, The Worst of War:

"I led his horse back home where they sat expecting him and I saw Mistis' and Master's hearts when they broke and that was the worst of war!"

Some heroes are unknown, unmourned, and consigned to oblivion because they had no bard to sing their praises. Determined that this would never happen to Sam, the hero of Sweetwater, the Pattons placed a marker in the family cemetery, which read: "SAM, Faithful to the end to those who trusted him."

The old burying ground lies hidden and forgotten along side the busy boulevard that leads into Florence from the east. Ruthless vandals have pulled over the large markers with heavy cables and removed forever the stone dedicated to Sam. Perhaps in the telling of this story to another generation it may be that the deeds of the old slave at Sweetwater will yet be remembered.

The Anecdote of The Officer's Party At Sweetwater

The story of East Florence's Sweetwater Plantation would not be complete without telling the colorful yarn of the Confederate General who stumbled into the water fountain at its front entrance. This embarrassing incident became a part of the lore of this great ante-bellum mansion as told by each generation of the family who lived there. The circumstances surrounding this event became the subject of mischievous banter as the hard-pressed soldiers made their way northward to the ill fated Battles of Franklin and Nashville.

The agonizing days of the terrible war were converging on an even more painful ending when Brigadier General Gideon Johnson Pillow used the manor house at Sweetwater for his headquarters. No doubt, Pillow's selection of Sweetwater for his headquarters was suggested by his military aide, Sergeant Robert Patton, who was later to die in the Battle of Selma. Young Robert was one of the three Patton boys in the Confederate Army.

Florence was overrun with soldiers in November, 1864. Confederate task forces had crossed the river at two places on October 30th to clear the town of its occupying

Federal garrison. Major General Nathan Bedford Forest arrived fifteen days later with some 3,000 cavalrymen to await the river crossing of General John Bell Hood's Army of Tennessee on November 15th with about 27,000 infantrymen and 2,000 cavalrymen. The historic north end of Court Street became Hood's general headquarters with some of his staff and general officers quartered in its stately residences. The divisions and brigades were camped in and around the city. The presence of a large military force in this small rural town was not new. Union General William Tecumseh Sherman, with his 15th U. S. Army Corps, had occupied Florence the previous November.

Sweetwater had been used by both Union and Confederate soldiers at various times through most of the war years. Until a few years ago, a long and well-defined earthen fortification could be seen along the slope of the cedar crest hill of the old McCorstin Plantation overlooking Sweetwater Avenue, an early stagecoach route into Florence from the east. The horse and plow obliterated similar fortifications made at Sweetwater within a few years following the war's end.

Gideon Pillow was one of the "political" generals of the Confederate Army. A graduate of the University of Nashville, he practiced law before and after the Civil War. In 1844, Pillow played a key role in getting his law partner, James K. Polk nominated for President of the United States. As a military officer, he rose to the rank of Major General in the Mexican War. However, fate was not on his side during the Civil War. The General's unfortunate role as second in command of Fort

Donelson at the time of its surrender plagued him for the remaining years of his life.

A Second Tract of Land Known As "Sweetwater"

There was another large tract of land east of Florence, which was known as "Sweetwater." Located at the mouth of Sweetwater Creek, it was described as "being on both sides of this branch." One of Florence's earliest water-powered mills, Andrews' Mill, was located on this property, near where today's Veterans Drive crosses over Sweetwater Creek. Patrick Andrews built a long race alongside Sweetwater Creek, which funneled the swift waters from the creek to turn the wheel that generated the power to operate the mill. Most of the late 19th century business and industry sections of East Florence were located on this large tract of land, which became known as the "Sweetwater Lands."

The deed to this tract was made out to Henry Smith in April 1827, by Patrick Andrews and his wife, Mary. The north boundary was referred to in this document as "the new Huntsville Road." This road had been constructed a year or two prior to 1827.

Another road mentioned in the deed was Circular Road, which was one of the boundary lines for Smith's Sweetwater tract. Circular Road was originally laid out by Ferdinand Sannoner to enclose the new town of Florence for military purposes. Royal Avenue was once a part of Sannoner's historic Circular Road.

Henry Smith, who purchased this land, referred to himself as "Henry Smith of Sweetwater" for the remaining years of his life. This man was one of Lauderdale County's largest landowners and probably the wealthiest man in the area prior to his death in 1846. He came from Halifax County, North Carolina, sometime before 1822. At that time, he acquired large land holdings in West Lauderdale County across from Koger Island. In 1826, he purchased a plantation known as "The Johnson Place" at where the Natchez Trace crosses the river. Other land in the west end of the county were bought in 1827. These sections of rich river bottoms were to become known as "Smithsonia." In addition to his farming enterprises, Henry Smith owed two ferries on the river and lots in the early river village of Smith's Point near the present Town of Riverton, in Colbert County.

Henry Smith married his first cousin, Mary, in Southhampton County, Virginia, in 1814. His second wife was also named Mary. Following the death of his second wife, Smith married Rebecca Beckwith, of the West Lauderdale County Beckwith Plantation, in 1842.

Smith died in 1846. He left a daughter, Anne Smith Darnell, and two grandchildren. His estate was inherited by this daughter and his grandchildren, nieces, nephews and friends. His first instruction to the executors of his estate was to procure a staff with a gold head upon which was to be inscribed: "Presented to Benjamine S. Jordan by his relative and friend, Henry Smith of Sweetwater, in token of his high regard and affection."

In December 1847, this Sweetwater property was advertised as a "sale of Sweetwater tract of land belonging to the estate of Henry Smith." This description of the land survived, and when the business section of East Florence came into being during the late 1880s, it carried with it the name "Sweetwater."

During his lifetime Henry Smith had provided for the education of a nephew, Henry D. Smith, whose imposing gravestone can be found in the center of a cotton field near the Gunwaleford Road in West Lauderdale County. Henry Smith removed this nephew from his will but was persuaded to reverse this only a few days prior to the elder Smith's death. The younger Henry D. Smith served in the Alabama legislature for a number of years. From early descriptions this nephew must have been rather tall and obese, as well as a colorful character. He earned a reputation at Montgomery for his sharp wit. This may have been why they called him "the razor strap man."

Henry D. Smith Cemetery West Of Florence

Where the owner of a large tract of land known as, Sweetwater, located at the mouth of Sweetwater Creek, is believed to be buried.

A Touch of Ireland in Ante-Bellum East Florence

None of the Old World countries were better represented in the early life of Florence than Ireland. These Celts made their mark as merchants; a few of them became Lauderdale County's wealthiest planters.

No Irishman was more Irish than Robert McCorstin who was hired as one of the bridge keepers for the first bridge across the Tennessee at Florence. Robert was born in

County Down, Ireland, in 1798. His wife Mary, born in 1807, was also a native of Ireland. Old-timers who remembered Robert and Mary were quick to recall their Irish brogue. Their accent always had the flavor of Ireland with little, if any, influence from the Americanized version of the English language. It was said, too, that the McCorstin home had the appearance of a small country estate in the green hills of Ireland.

The McCorstins must have been a family of some means. In 1839 the same year the river bridge was completed they purchased 305 acres of land from Judge John McKinley of the U.S. Supreme Court. In the deed it was noted that "the said McCorstin is now erecting a brick house." This story-and-a-half structure was located on a high ridge overlooking Sweetwater Creek. Its walls were of solid brick made from the red clay mined at the site. There was a large entrance hall with stairs leading to the bedrooms above. Large fireplaces were at each end of the house. In addition to the main entrance there were two other front doors, one to the parlor and the other leading to the dining room. At the foot of the hill below, the house was a large spring that served the family. Later in the early 1890's this same spring, known then as Simpson Spring, was harnessed to supply water to the Cherry Cotton Mill and Village located a short distance to the south in Sweetwater Creek Valley.

The McCorstin land was sandwiched between two large East Florence ante-bellum tracts of land both called "Sweetwater." To the northeast, at the head of Sweetwater Creek, was the large Sweetwater Plantation of Robert Miller Patton who briefly served as Governor of Alabama in 1865. The Wilson Dam Reservation and most of the Weeden Heights section of East Florence were later carved from these Patton lands.

To the south, and near the mouth of Sweetwater Creek, was the second tract of land. Henry Smith who until his dying day referred to himself as "Henry Smith of Sweetwater" owned this land. Most of the industrial and business sections of East Florence were located on these Sweetwater lands of Henry Smith.

During the Civil War, the McCorstin property became a campsite at various times for both Union and Confederate soldiers. Until recent years a long and deep trench curved around the crest of the hill overlooking Sweetwater Avenue then, a major thoroughfare into the city from the east. In early November, 1864, while General Hood was in Florence, the McCorstin house, according to an old veteran of the Battles of Franklin and Nashville, was used as headquarters by his "general." It is believed this officer was either the one-armed Major General William Wing "Old Blizzards" Loring or Brigadier General Mark P. Lowrey. Both were in the area and both were in command of troops from Mississippi and Alabama.

Robert McCorstin died in January, 1865, some three months before the war ended. Mary had preceded him in death by some nineteen years. Their estate was sold in 1870 to John H. Price, who in 1877, sold it to Robert Simpson. Afterwards, the McCorstin home site became known as the "Simpson Place," and later, it was called the "Gray Place."

This historic landmark of East Florence was destroyed in 1954 to make way for a large shopping center that was being built on the newly opened Florence Boulevard. At the same time the McCorstin Cemetery, located at the present site of the state garage on State Street also disappeared. However, the beautiful marble obelisk grave marker for Robert and Mary McCorstin was removed from the small plot and placed in a vacant section of the Confederate "Soldiers Rest" Burial Grounds in the Florence Cemetery.

The story of the McCorstins and their farmhouse overlooking Sweetwater Creek is but a small chapter of the rich history of all the Irish immigrants in early Florence. These folk left a legacy remembered as a touch of Ireland among the hills of North Alabama.

Florence's Civil War Military Fort

Today's popular Florence Lauderdale Coliseum was yesterday's old Civil War Military Fort. It served both the Union and Confederate Armies, depending upon which one was occupying North Alabama at the time. Long trenches of earthworks once lined the crest of this high palisade overlooking the river below. These had been erected for two purposes: to protect the town and to prevent the passing of federal gunboats over the Muscle Shoals. From here, the artillerymen in these breastworks had a commanding view of the river from Tuscumbia Landing upstream to Campbell's Ferry above Florence.

In February 1862, following the capitulation of Forts Donelson and Henry at the strategic entrances to the Cumberland and Tennessee Rivers more than 500 sick and wounded Confederate soldiers were sent by boats to improvised military hospitals in downtown Florence. It was imperative to secure these patients as far inside the Confederate lines as possible; Florence was as far up the Tennessee as these transports could reach because of the treacherous shoals in the river. Confederate General Albert Sidney Johnson placed Brigadier General Daniel Ruggles, a West Point officer and veteran of the Seminole and Mexican Wars, in charge of the defense of Florence. This soldier, who had just reached his 53rd birthday, was born in Barre, Massachusetts.

The presence of this high-ranking Yankee in the Southern Army infuriated General Grant who at least on one occasion used sarcastic references as to Ruggles' abilities as a commander. Ruggles, with his flowing white beard, could be seen galloping over the streets of Florence for weeks on end as he supervised the erection of fortifications around the perimeter of the town. The Old Fort on the present grounds of the Colliseum became key to his defense of the town from the Union Navy.

Because of its location, the Old Fort played important roles in a number of river crossings by both armies throughout the war years. Its most frequent occupant was Moulton native, Brigadier General Philip Dale Roddey, who was known as the "Defender of North Alabama." Early in 1863 he made quite a name for himself by repairing boats for the Confederate Navy at the Florence Port. It was Roddey who raised the Confederate Dunbar at the Gunwale Ford on Cypress Creek and floated it over the Shoals to the upper reaches of the Tennessee River.

Colonel George Gibbs Dribrell of General Forrest's command placed his Huggins Artillery Battery on these heights in the spring of 1863.

On one occasion, his large cannons fired across the river into South Florence. This caused the alarmed citizens there to wave white sheets and tablecloths along the riverbank! The nearest enemy was General Greenville Dodge who, upon hearing the sounds of Gibbs' guns, quickly withdrew his forces from Tuscumbia.

The last military action against the Old Fort was Christmas 1864. This was when Union Admiral S. P. Lee was maneuvering his two gunboats over the Shoals in an attempt to cut off General Hood's retreat at the Bainbridge Ferry east of Florence. While passing below the Old Fort he fired several volleys into its vacant earthworks apparently as a safety precaution.

Time and bulldozers have erased even the last vestige of the Old Confederate Fort. Yet, the commanding overlook from this strategic wartime place remains as one of the most scenic views along the mighty Tennessee River.

When the Whistles Blew it was Big News

During the early days at Florence, the bells at the Presbyterian and Methodist Churches were used as a means for calling out the militia and fire bridges. Sometimes they were rung as a media to announce the happenings of something significant locally or nationally or around the world.

When large industries came to East Florence in the latter part of the Nineteenth Century, the Church bells gave way to the stream whistles of the local factories. Old timers enjoy talking about the various sound of these whistles. They say that it was easy to identify which of the shrill sounds came from the wagon factory, stave mills, stove foundry, cotton mills, or the knitting mill.

At special occasions, church bells from across the city joined the industrial whistles in celebration, such as New Year's Eve, the signing of the armistice at the end of World War I, and the surrender of Germany and Japan in World War II. These sounds seem to have left indelible images among those who lived in that era and knew the excitement of those clarion calls.

Charlie Brown was one of those with a remarkable memory of these whistles. Born on Cherry Hill at East Florence in 1917, Charlie could not remember World War I, and was away in the Army during World War II. Yet, he had an almost incredible recollection of a Spring day in 1927 when it seemed to him the whole world was filled with the soundings of factory whistles.

Charlie, or "C.D." as he was sometimes called, was chopping cotton for his older brother, Melvin, on that memorable date in late, Spring. Melvin had rented the field where the Florence-Lauderdale Coliseum is located. This was once a prized Civil War historical site before the coming of the bulldozers. A well-defined earthwork ran across the crest of this hill. Its purpose was to protect Florence from both gunboats and Yankee invaders from the river below the town. It was used as well by the Yankees for the same purpose during the times they were in control of the north bank of the Tennessee. Unusually large trees shaded the trench and were, perhaps, four or five feet in diameter when cut down to make way for the coliseum. C.D. and his brother, Melvin, would eat their sack lunches under this massive canopy of limbs while dangling their feet over the side of this earthen fortification. Following these lunch breaks, the Brown brothers would often gather a pocket of minie balls from the trench to be used later as sinkers for fishing poles.

It was on an eventful day, May 21, 1927, when the whistles blew. From across the hills could be heard the sounds from the Florence Wagon Works, Cherry Cotton Mill, and the other factories scattered about Florence. Then came the nearby shrills from Ashcraft Cotton Mill. Dropping their hoes and rushing to the crest of the hill, C.D. and Melvin saw people running from their homes and into the streets of the village. Everybody, it seemed, was heading toward G. S. Mitchell's Grocery Store on Park Street. Mitchell's Store had one of the less than 1,500 telephones in Florence, and his place of business was looked upon as a "place to get the news." There were very few radios in those days as the introduction of radio broadcasting had occurred only six years previously.

The telegraph and telephone were the two major local ties to the outside world.

When C.D. and Melvin reach Mitchell's Store they were greeted by shouts that "Lindberg had landed in Paris, France!" Charles A. Lindberg had left New York on May 20th, and for thirty-three-and half lonely hours had made his solo flight across the Atlantic in his "Spirit of St. Louis."

The nation had waited and wondered if he could do the impossible. Some doubted while others prayed.

The world changed that day. It would never be the same again. It was not for Charles David Brown either. He had witnessed many events and seen many places. Yet, he had never been far from that memory of his brother's cotton patch and the sounds of those factory whistles.

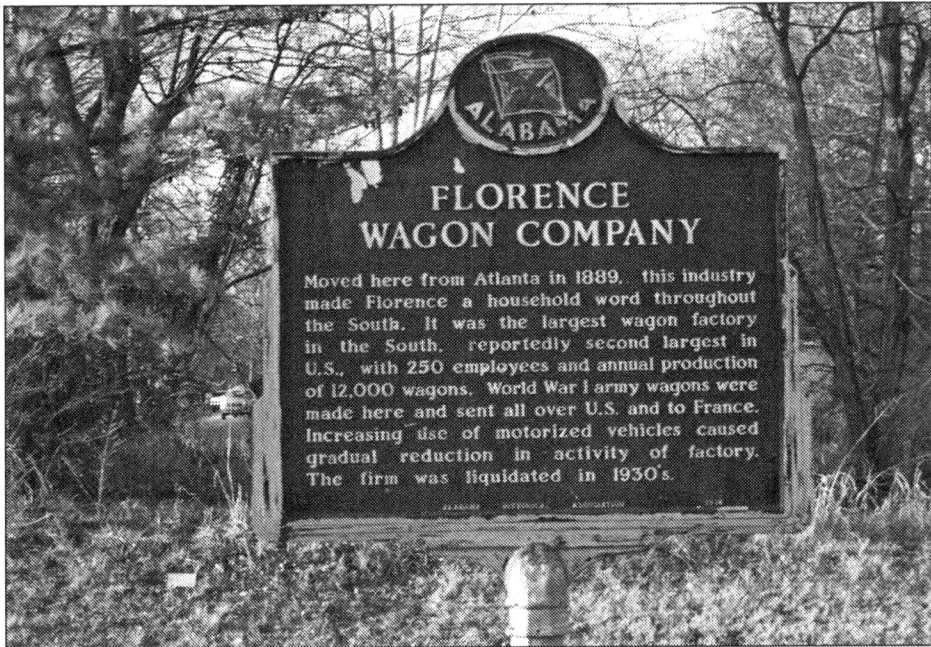

FLORENCE WAGON COMPANY

Moved here from Atlanta in 1889, this industry made Florence a household word throughout the South. It was the largest wagon factory in the South, reportedly second largest in U.S., with 250 employees and annual production of 12,000 wagons. World War I army wagons were made here and sent all over U.S. and to France. Increasing use of motorized vehicles caused gradual reduction in activity of factory. The firm was liquidated in 1930's.

Mills

— The Industrial Section of Florence —
Sweetwater

Founders Saw Creek's Importance

The founders of Florence were quick to point out the advantages of "the small but beautiful creek of Sweetwater (which) winds along near the outskirts of town." As early as 1822, Gen. John Coffee, James Jackson and, Edward Ward began the construction of a cotton mill along Sweetwater Creek near what is now the Huntsville Road bridge.

Ferdinand Sannoner showed what might have been this vacant building in 1852 as a "future factory site." Although this early cotton mill was short-lived, it was a forerunner of the cotton factories that were later to identify Florence with the Southern textile industries.

Upstream from the present Patton Street bridge over Sweetwater Creek is the site where Coffee and a silent partner, President Andrew Jackson, built an experimental cotton hulling mill in 1832. Coffee and others had previously made investments in a small factory at this same site. A short distance downstream from the site of the Coffee-Jackson cotton-hulling mill is the site of an early grist mill built by another prominent American, U.S. Supreme Court Associate Justice John McKinley. The judge sold this mill site, along with the adjoining 305 acres in 1839 to the Irishman Robert McCorstine.

As early as 1852, Patrick Andrews was operating a grist mill on Sweetwater Creek near the present crossing of Veterans Drive. Andrews' Dam was located upstream from Huntsville Road, requiring the digging of a long race to funnel the water to the wheel that turned the machinery at the mill.

Sweetwater Creek became a major industrial water source during the East Florence Boom of the late 19th century. The Cherry Cotton Mill was built alongside its bank in 1893. A chestnut log dam behind the mill supplied a pool of water that fed the steam boiler, which supplied the power to operate the machinery in the factory. The drinking and fire-protection water for the Cherry Mill was originally piped from Simpson Spring, located near the intersection of Sweetwater Avenue and Patton Street. Later after the Weeden Heights community was developed, potable water was piped there from nearby Sweetwater Spring.

Sweetwater Creek flowed through the heavy industrialized section of East Florence that was located south of Huntsville Road during the later part of the 19th and early part of the 20th centuries.

In this area were two of the large iron furnaces, along with other mills and factories. Great piles of slag dominated the creek bank in this area until it was learned that this byproduct could successfully be used in the, manufacture of building blocks. The new corridor across the Patton Island Bridge, changes forever the appearance of what has been the saga of "the small but beautiful creek of Sweetwater". However, its story will be indelibly woven into the fabric that tells the history of Florence.

A Short Cut to East Florence

Blasting commenced on Maxwell Hill during the week ending January 11, 1890. This was a victorious occasion for the new industries that were locating or were planning to locate in East Florence. It was especially good news for the plant workers and their families who were already making their homes in this unique industrial section of town. In less than three years, the population of Florence had expanded from about 1,400 to more than 6,000, mostly as a result the East Florence Boom. Maxwell Hill formed a high and steep barrier between Florence and East Florence. Although there was an early walking trail that descended this steep slope that could sometimes be used by horses, it was necessary for vehicular traffic to and from the newly developed industrial area of town to travel north on Royal Avenue to the old Circular Road (now Grady Lyles Drive) and enter Florence from what is now Hermitage Drive. Royal Avenue had been graded and improved in the spring of 1887. Later improvements to Royal Avenue included the installation of a concrete culvert in a deep ditch, which ran alongside this thoroughfare between North Florence and East Florence. Captain Robert Andrews, the long-time mayor of Florence, announced in January 1890, that a deep cut would be made through Maxwell Hill to join East Tennessee Street with Royal Avenue, thus providing a short cut to East Florence as well as to open a new entrance into Florence from the east. A depth of seventeen feet had to be cut and blasted from the hill to provide the proper grade required for vehicular traffic. Most of the dirt and rocks removed from the hill were used to fill a wide and deep depression that existed between the east entrance to the City Cemetery and Maxwell Hill. (The continuation of this same depression is visible today in the east side of the Florence Cemetery.) For a number of years this extension of East Tennessee Street was called

"Maxwell Cut." Later, it became known as "Tennessee Cut".

The Industrial Section of Florence Called Sweetwater

(View of the industrial section 1900)

The industrial revolution that swept across the nation in the 1880's made its dramatic appearance at Florence in 1887. It was called the "East Florence Boom", and became the most successful industrial period of the history of Florence. More industry was located at Florence from 1887 until about 1910 than during all the other years of its history, before and after. One writer, visiting the city in 1903, noted that there was a solid line of industry in East Florence that stretched some two miles alongside the Tennessee River. The population of the city jumped

500 percent, from 1,600 to 6,000 people, in a three-year span.

The money behind the East Florence Boom came from investors, principally it is believed, from the Northeastern states. There is suspicion that Andrew Carnegie and Andrew Mellon financed some of the capital outlay. It is known that there was a Mellon connection at Florence through the Negley family.

There was also a Tiffany connection at Florence in those years. One of the heirs to the world-famous jeweler was connected with the L&N Railroad in East Florence. He was a bachelor and boarded in the home of Dr. James Brock at what is now the northwest corner of Dr. Hicks Boulevard and South Pine Street. "Tiffy", as he was called by the Brock family, was a colorful character about town. It was said that his family was responsible for his assignment to Florence, a great distance from the family business in New York, because of his addiction to "strong drink".

Early Iron Furnaces at East Florence

Good, honest, hard work! But proud and grateful to be a part of the labor force that made Sweetwater a thriving industrial section of Florence during the late 20th century.

The W.B. Wood Furnace was one of the first of the "East Florence Boom" industries. Its construction, alongside Sweetwater Creek near Veterans Drive, began in 1888, under the guiding hand of John M. Norton.

John Norton, native of Brownsville, Pennsylvania, was employed by Judge Wood to oversee the completion of the furnace. He came from an iron industry family. His father, George W. Norton, was the pioneer nail manufacturer of the Ohio Valley. At the time of George's death in 1886, he was the president and principal owner of the Belfonte Iron Works at Ironton, Ohio.

It was said that John W. Norton was only nine years of age when he began the trade of nail maker at his father's

Belfonte Iron Works. After a number of years, John was made superintendent of the Belfonte Iron Works in Wheeling, West Virginia. Here he, unfortunately, was caught under a locomotive and lost one of his legs.

Later in life, he constructed the Norton Iron Works at Ashland, Kentucky. Prior to being employed at the East Florence plant by Judge Wood, Norton was superintendent of the Alabama, Tennessee, Coal and Iron Works at Sheffield. While residing at Florence, Norton and his wife were active in the First United Methodist Church where he served on the Board of Stewards.

The W. B. Wood Furnace was later incorporated by the Florence Cotton and Iron Company in January 1889. Norton completed the furnace in 1891, and was made its general manager. The company had a rated capacity of 45,000 tons output a year. This industry fell victim to the 1892 depression, however, and was sold to the Sheffield Steel and Iron Company in 1899. Considerable remodeling and upgrading was undertaken, and when the furnace resumed operation in 1901, it produced at a rate of, 70,000 tons a year. Its smokestack was the highest of any in the entire area. The furnace operated three shifts a day, and at night when it's slag was dumped alongside the railroad track its red glow lit up the surrounding countryside. A number of stories were told about this spectacular sight. One, as remembered, was an Irishman, Pat McClutchin, who had just arrived in East Florence. He was aroused from his sleep about midnight by the bright glow from the slag. His loud moans disturbed the other guests in the Kiddy Hotel. It was said that Pat thought he had died and was entering the gates of Hell. This furnace remained in operation unit 1926.

Another iron industry, the North Alabama Furnace, was opened in October 1889. This facility was built on twenty-five acres of land bordering the old Muscle Shoals Canal. It measured 75 feet by 16 feet and had an annual output of 30,000 tons. Its basic raw materials consisted of Hematite ore from Tennessee and coke manufactured in Alabama and Virginia. The company was sold to the Spathite Iron Company the following year. The new owner rebuilt the furnace and began production in 1894. The iron produced was of such excellent quality that it sold for as much as $0.50 to $ 1.00 per ton higher than pig iron. Due to its high production costs, however, the furnace was shut down in the spring, of 1895.

There was a third iron furnace, known as "Little Lady", at Florence during this era. However, it was located on South Wood Avenue, and was not a part of the East Florence Industry.

Judge William B. Wood

Judge William Basil Wood was perhaps the most instrumental personality behind the industrial boom that came to Sweetwater in the late 1880's.

Born at Nashville, Tennessee, in 1820, Wood moved to Florence at an early age. His father, Alexander H. Wood, became Florence's first mayor after the city was incorporated in 1826. Following his graduation from historic LaGrange College, William Basil Wood was admitted to the bar at Florence in 1843. He was later elected Judge of Lauderdale County Court, and returned to this position after serving as a Colonel in the Confederate Army during the war years.

In addition to his professional duties, Wood became a leader in a number of private enterprises. Prior to the war he was engaged in the manufacture of woolens, and was principal owner of a line of steamboats, which plied the Tennessee, Ohio and Mississippi rivers. After the war, Wood turned his attention to railroads, serving as president of a number of these early organizations.

It was through his position as President of the Florence Land Mining and Manufacturing Company that Wood was able to promote the development of East Florence in what was known as the Florence Boom. Thus, men such as William Basil Wood, Thomas Jefferson Phillips, and Nial C. Elting became the founders who brought Sweetwater into being.

These row houses once stood alongside what is now Veteran's Drive on East Hill. They were owned by the Philadelphia Furnace and were homes for the iron workers at the mill.

The Foundry

The Foundry, located on Commerce Street, is one of the surviving 19th century industries. It is owned and operated by the heirs of, A. R. Tomlinson, III, of Florence.

Originally known as the Stove Works, it was relocated to Florence, in 1888 from Evansville, Indiana, to become the Florence Stove and Manufacturing Company. It was owned and operated by Henry H. Theole. Thomas J. Phillips was one of the investors in the company. In the early days, the 150,000 square foot foundry produced stoves, heaters, wash pots, skillets, "sad" irons for pressing clothes, and "dog" irons for fireplaces. These products were shipped to various parts of Alabama and Tennessee. Theole also established a specialty of machine and jobbing work, repairing, brass and iron molding and pattern work. Several ex-slaves were employed in the casting department and made a name for themselves as a result of their talent. Sets of dog irons made by Pompeii are on display in the City of Florence's W.C. Handy Library.

There was a row of company-owned red frame houses for the workers that were lined up along the street south of the foundry known, as the "Theole Row".

At one time convicts were employed as operators and workers in the foundry.

Charles Martin and his brother, William Martin, Sr., purchased the business in 1918 and renamed it The Martin Stove and Range Company. Within six months they had turned the failing foundry into a profit-making enterprise. The family expanded its operations into Martin Industries in 1987.

In recent years the late A. R. Tomlinson, III, established, The Foundry as an independent casting producer for original equipment manufactures. It heats 2,000-degree molten scrap and pig iron that is poured into molds produced at the site. The Foundry also supplies patterns, machining and assembling, painting, plating, and heat-treating. In 1987, the annual payroll was $1.5 million with sales amounting to $5 million from more than 10,000 tons of gray iron castings.

The Foundry

The Florence Wagon Works

The advent of the two nitrate plants in Colbert County during World War I and the political scenes associated with the building of Wilson Dam following the war made the name "Muscle Shoals" a household word across the nation.

However, the name, "Florence", was already well known as a result of the popular "Light Running Florence" wagons being produced at East Florence.

The Florence Wagon Works moved to Florence from Atlanta, Georgia, in 1889. It was first organized in, Atlanta, by, Dr. A. D. Bellamy and his father. Dr. Bellamy, moved it to Alabama to be near to the hardwood timber that was so plentiful in the foothills of the Appalachians. The company increased its capital when reorganizing for its relocation, and Dr. Bellamy was elected president. Other managers were: D. H. Turnbull, D. B. Turnbull, Thomas B. Ingram, E. H. Melling, A. B. Mason, E. Lyon, John T. Little, Clifford Hollman, Jake Hollman, Thomas Pickens, and M. H. Princehouse.

It became one of the largest industries in the area, and during its peak, employed about 175 people. The plant covered 15 acres near the old Muscle Shoals Canal at a place known locally as "East Hill". The Magnolia Church of Christ was built on this site in 2002. In addition to the availability of water transportation, a railroad spur also served it. The management provided a number of company-owned houses for employees. It had its own power plant and fire protection devices that included an automatic sprinkler system, fire hoses, and fire brigade. The motto, "Nothing Is Too Good For The Florence", was used throughout the plant and village.

Nearby Mooloosa Spring was used for potable water for the employees. As a young boy Shaler S. Roberts, Sr. was employed as the water boy. He later became a well-known Florence physician. The early Indians used Moolooosa Spring for its mineral waters. About the turn of the century, the water from this spring was bottled and sold in downtown Florence as well as in other nearby towns for its advertised health benefits.

The Florence Wagon Works became the second largest producer of wagons, second only to the Studebaker Company, which later made a name for itself in the automobile business. Two million feet of hardwood was consumed annually. From 10,000 to 15,000 "Light

Running Florence" wagons a year were produced and shipped. This popular wagon could be seen from Maryland to California and in Mexico. During the Spanish American War they could be found in Cuba. In World War I the Florence wagon went with the American forces to Europe.

Near the beginning of the new 20th Century, the management of the factory changed hands. Florence attorney, John T. Ashcraft of the prominent cotton mill family, became its new chief executive officer. The old Florence Hotel on South Court Street, built in 1888, was purchased and used as a display "show" room for the wagons. At this time the main executive suites of the factory were moved to this and other locations near downtown Florence. This building later became well known as the Lamar Furniture Company site.

The arrival of the automobile, tractor and truck diminished the need for horse-drawn vehicles. During its final years the company turned to lawn chairs, swings, and other furniture. The last remains of the Florence Wagon Works were moved to Hickory, North Carolina, and by 1941 its doors in East Florence were closed forever.

The Lumber yard at the Florence Wagon Factory covered several acres. (This lumber was air dried prier to its use in the manufacturing of wagons.)

It was said that there could have been no better place anywhere, timber-wise, than North Alabama for the location of a wagon factory. The hills and hollows of this area were great producers of hard woods of every kind.

The wagon wheel shop workers proudly display the way, the wheels that are to be assembled on the famous Florence wagons. The hubs were made from local white oak and the spokes were from Alabama hickory. Alonzo Lindsey was foreman of the wheel shop. Mr. Cagle, who was both deaf and mute, took charge of the wheels after they were completed.

A general store in Amory, Mississippi, with advertisement signs which designated it as an outlet for the Florence wagons.

The Light Florence Running Wagon became a household word across the nation, and especially in Texas and other points out west. The employees at the wagon factory took great pride in their work. Long after the factory had closed its doors its former employees were still bragging about being apart of this industry. A hundred years following its initial operation, descendants of its employees gathered at the Broadway Recreation Center in East Florence for their annual Florence Wagon Factory Reunion.

YOU HAVE TRIED THE REST
NOW BUY THE BEST

Made and
Guaranteed
By

FLORENCE WAGON CO., Florence, Ala.

The Light Florence Running Wagon from 10,000 to 15,000 annually produced and shipped.

The Florence Wagon Works transport wagon, above, was driven by Albert Lindsey. Emory McDonald, Sr., is in front and Jake Hollman stands near the rear.

Managers and Employees of the Wagon Factory

This list of managers and workers from 1889-1941 who made the Florence Light Running Wagons famous was compiled in 1980 by O. C. Phillips, James D. Beadle and L. D. Staggs, Jr.

Those who remember the workers who came and went for a period of some thirty or forty years base it upon recollections. Unfortunately, there are missing names due to the long time span from the closing of the plant to the decade of the 1980's.

Abernathy	Collier, W. I.
Adams, Lee	Couch
Angel	Cox, Chester
Arnett, Dena Smith	Craig, Charlie

Arnett, Samuel
Ashcraft, John T.
(President 1905)
Barnes, Leo
Bellamy, A. D.
(President 1889)
Brewer, Neal
Broadfoot
Brown, Walker
Baker, Luther
(Bookkeeper)
Barnes, Pink
Beadle, David
Beckman, Michael
Bender, Mary Douglass
(Secretary)
Bevis, Jones
Bevis
Biggers, Kelly
Biggers
Billingsley
Blakely, Ray Miller, Sr.
Bonds, Charlie
Bonds, Fred
Bonds, John
Boston
Brewer, Grover Cleveland
Brewer, Hester
Cagle
Fields, Hershel
Finney, J. W.
(Sales Manager)

Craig, Glenn Clifton
Creel, George
Crunk
Curtis
Daily, George
Daily, John
Dendy, Jim
Dendy, Pete
Dendy, Pruitt
Deeds, E. L.
(Salesman)
Douglas, Albert
Douglas, Sterling
Eastep, Jesse
Eastep, Will
Edwards, D. J.
Edwards, J. T.
(Lumber Buyer)
Evans, Will
Faulkner, John
Fields, Charles
Hensley, Milton
Hicks, Bert
Hewitt, Leslie
Hill, Frank
Hill, Wilmer
Floyd, G. D.
(Salesman)
Freeman, Miles
Fritts
Futrell, Babe
Futrell, John

Fisher, Sam
Flippo
Cagle Canerday
Carter, Edward R.
(Master Mechanic)
Carter, John Henry
Clayton, Harvey
Cole, Percy
Cole, Reuben
Hallman, Clifford
(Superintendent)
Hollman, Jacob M. "Jake"
(Foreman)
Halls
Hardiman, Stanley
Hardiman, William
Harlan, Samuel
(Management)
Hawkins, Jack
Hendon, Arthur
Henley, Earnest W.
(Cashier)
Hensley, Guy
Lindsey, Leonard
Little, John T
(Management)
Lyon, Ed
(Office Manager)
Martin
Mason, A. B.
(Management)
McDonald, Jones Emory, Sr.

Gamble, Tom
Garrett, Sam
Geise, Johnny
Gist
Green, John Thomas
Green, Morgan
Grigsby, Bertha
Hale, Brandon
Hale, Claborrn
Kirby, Horace
Knight
Landrum, Andrew
Lanier, Louis "Little"
Lanier, Louis "Large"
LaMay, William
(Foreman of Wheel)
Lindsey, Albert
Lindsey, Alonzo
Lindsey, Chester
Lindsey, Edward
Lindsey, John
Rickard, Hunter
Rickard, Oscar
Rickard, Price
Rickard, Rome
Rickard, Timothy
Rickard, F. A. (or Fred)
Richardson, Brandon
Risner, Dick
Risner, John
Risner, Reed
Roach

McDonald, Jesse W. "Will"
McDonald, W. Ervin
Melling, E. A.
(Salesman)
McFall
McGee
McKinney, John
Milner, E. A.
Mobley
Hodges, Chester
Hodges, Wilson
Hopkins, John
Hyde, Lando
Ingram, Thomas B.
(Management)
James, Arthur
James, Eugene
James, Hugh
Jones, Calvin
Kennedy
Kershaw, Charlie
Kershaw, Robert
Stricklin, Howard
Stutts, Arthur
Swinea
Terrell, Andrew
Terrell, Sam
Thigpen
Tolliver
Tucker, Frank
Turnbull, D. B.
(Management)

Robert, Dendy
Robert, Logan
Robert, Jimmy
Roberts, John
Morgan, Bob
Mueller
Nelson, Thomas
Nichols, Webster "Web"
Owens
Parrish, Edward
Peden, Henry
Perryman, Arthur "Red"
Pickens, Thomas
(Management)
Ramsey, Lawrence
Rauls
Redding, Thompson
Reynolds, Thomas
Reynolds, Will
Rickard, David
Rickard, Emmett
Rickard, Fred
Smith, Amos
Smith, John
Smith
Stafford, Ervin
Stafford, S. E.
(Paint Foreman)
Staggs, Lester D., Sr
Stewart, Columbus
Vessell, Floyd E.
Vessell, Luther

Turnbull, D. H.
(Management)
Turner
Turner
Vessell, Dent
Roberts, Shaler S., Sr.
Romine, James
Sanderson, Albert
Sanderson, Arthur
Sanderson, John
Sharpston, Willis
Shelton, Felix
Shook, Bill
Simmons, Boone
Sims, Herschel
Slaughter

Waldrop
Ware, William
Watson, Albert
Watson, Robert
White, Felix
Wylie, Bill
Willford, Claude
(Purchasing Agent)
Walker, Frank
Wilkes, George W.
Williams
Williams
Wisdom
Woody, Enoch
Woody, George

Descriptions of some of the above employees and their duties as remembered by James D. Beadle (in interview with author, July 25, 1987.)

Dave Beadle was called a utility man; he was able to operate any machine in the wood shop and did a lot of the bench work. At times he was assigned as night watchman and occasionally tended the fire in the huge boiler.

Alonzo Lindsey, who lived near the Wagon Works, was in charge of the hub department. His daughter, Elsie, was employed as secretary at the Wagon Factory following her graduation from college. She later became a school teacher.

Calvin Jones worked in the hub department.

Walker Brown was yard foreman and was responsible for seeing that only the best grade white oak and hickory were used in the making of the spokes.

George Daily, a Baptist preacher and Watkins salesman, was employed in the Wagon Factory to file and repair saws.

Leonard Lindsey, who later became an East Florence merchant, filed and repaired saws.

George Wilkes, a Methodist preacher, was a master mechanic. His daughter, Mildred, began her career as a business and professional secretary, at the Florence Wagon Factory.

Jones Emory McDonald, Sr., was a timber buyer. It was said that he could ride by a forest and estimate the board feet it contained without getting out of his wagon.

Frank Hill is shown on the third row above (extreme left). He was foreman over the woodworking department and lived on Catholic Hill.

Kneeling on the front row (far right) is Hardy Perryman. His daughter, Loretta Pittman, was one of the most beloved and popular teachers at Brandon School. Second from right, front row, is Rome Rickard. He was employed in the wheel department and also served as a lay preacher at St. James United Methodist.

The Proud And The Loyal

It would be hard to find a more loyal group of employees than those who proudly proclaimed that they were workers at the Florence Wagon factory. Many of them are shown in the photograph above. The factory at one time employed 175 people.

Identification of a few in the photograph above: Frank Carter is fourth from the left on the front row. Frank was choir director for St. James United Methodist Church for many years.

Seventh from right on front row is Thompson "Thompse" Redding a great-grandson of William Reading who was with General Mad Anthony Wayne at Yorktown when Lord Cornwallis surrendered to General George Washington during the American Revolution. Hunter Rickard, a nephew of Thompse Redding, is seated fourth from the right on the third row.

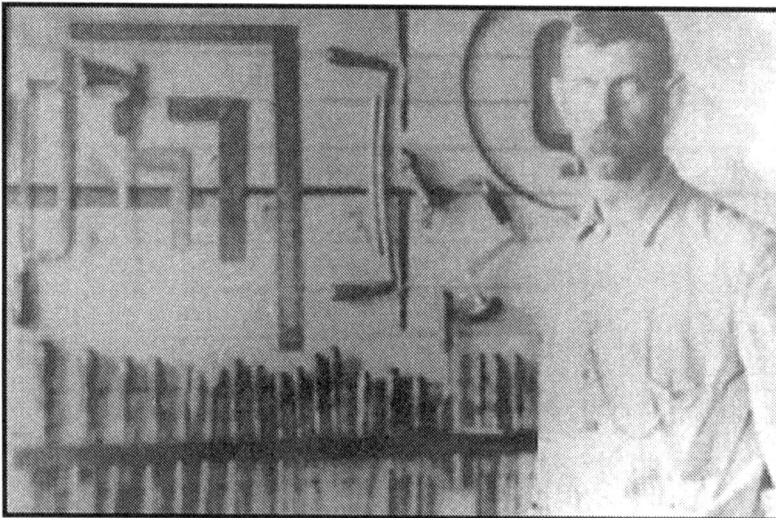

The Reverend George Wilkes, Master Mechanic, shown in his shop on site at the Florence Wagon Factory about 1915. Wilkins served as pastor of a number of Methodist churches.

Pictured above are the executives of the Wagon Factory about 1905: Ed Lynn, Claude Wilford, Edward R. Carter, D. J. Edwards, J. M. Hallman, E. S. Foote, E. L. Deeds, John T. Ashcraft, S. D. Floyd, E. A. Milner, E. W. Henley, Will LeMay, S. E. Stafford and Robert Morgan, Jr.

The East Florence Cotton Industry

Florence was established as a river town because of its strategic location at the foot of the Muscle Shoals. Soon, however, because of its abundance of water and numerous falling streams it became a cotton mill town. An 1832 map showed a cotton factory on Sweetwater Creek.

Cherry Cotton Mill

On January 4, 1893, the Mountain Mills Company was incorporated as the Cherry Cotton Mill, and moved to the bank of Sweetwater Creek near the site of an 1832 cotton factory. The new officers were: Colonel N. F. Cherry, Nial C. Elting and Charles M. Brandon.

The relocated mill took the name of its principal stockholder, Colonel Noel Franklin Cherry. Born June 1, 1831, he was a son of a wealthy cotton planter, Eli Cherry, of Hardin County, Tennessee. The name Cherry is well known to scholars of the Battle of Shiloh. General Grant was staying at the Cherry Mansion in Savannah Tennessee, when he received news that General Albert Sidney Johnston had attacked his forces encamped at nearby Pickwick Landing the beginning of the Battle of Shiloh.

Colonel Cherry, although reared on a farm, began his career in the mercantile business. He later moved to McNairy County, Tennessee where he lived more than twenty years. From there he moved to Corinth, Mississippi, and then to Florence so as to oversee the cotton factory operations that he and his brother had established at Mountain Mills near Barton in Colbert County. He and his wife, Francis Keturah Johnson Cherry, made their home in a large white Victorian mansion on North Wood Avenue. They had five children: The Reverend J. W. Cherry, Dr. E. O. Cherry, H. A. Cherry, Mrs. R. M. Martin and Miss Margaret Cherry. Colonel Cherry, a loyal and faithful member of Florence's First United Methodist Church, died in October 1903 at the age of 73 years. He is buried in the Florence Cemetery.

Nial Childs Elting was a native of Ellenville, New York. It was the East Florence Boom that brought him to Florence in 1889 to establish, along with R. L. Bliss, the First National Bank. He died April 16, 1933. He and his wife, Annie Van Sickler, had no heirs. She died in 1905. They are buried in the Florence Cemetery. Elting bequeathed to his church, The First Presbyterian Church of Florence, the income from a liberal trust fund.

Charles M. Brandon was the son of Washington M. and Mary B. Brandon. His father was the superintendent of the railroad bridge at Florence. Charles M. Brandon was never married. He was responsible for the location of Brandon Elementary School at East Florence. This school was named in his memory the year following his death, which occurred October 26, 1898 at Ashville, North Carolina. His body was returned to his home and he is buried in the Florence Cemetery.

The managers of the mill built company houses on nearby Cherry Hill for its employees. A number of private homes were built in Sweetwater Creek Valley by employees of the mill, as well as by employees of other East Florence industry. Life in the village was fairly well regulated, time-wise, by the loud steam whistle that announced the beginning and ending of the workday as well as the time for the lunch break. By 1903, Cherry Cotton Mill had a capacity of 12,000 spindles and employed some 400 people. These workers were classified as spinners, spoolers, twisters, reelers, doffers, and sweepers. Mechanics were employed to keep the machines running. Payroll records dated April, 1898 listed a scale of wages ranging from 15 cents to 75 cents a day for most of the 400 employees. The mechanics and other craftsmen earned from $1.00 to $1.50 a day. The highest wage listed was that of Franklin Pierce Johnson at $2.00 a day. He was classified as a supervisor. A newspaper article in September 1936 reported a total of 300 workers and an annual payroll amounting to $225,000. Officers at that time were: Jewett T. Flagg, President, Miles W. Darby, Vice- President, Sam C. Harlan, Treasurer, and Frank Longcrier, Assistant Treasurer. Fred Gamble was listed as a mill foreman. Miles Darby, who came to Florence from Mississippi as a boy, served as Vice-President and General Manager for 44 years. From 1893 until the beginning of the Great Depression in 1929, the Cherry Cotton Mill had consumed approximately 150,000 bales of cotton, most of which was grown by farmers in Lauderdale and surrounding counties. Quality cotton yarns were shipped all over the United States and into several foreign countries. However, this once prosperous cotton factory was not able to survive the financial crisis brought about by the Great Depression.

Cherry Cotton Mill Employees (1930)

Old timers remembered that the Cherry Cotton Mill was "blowed out" in August 1893 by Tom Anderton. This meant that Tom Anderton, the boiler man, had brought the steam boiler to a full head and, for the first time the power generated by the boiler was converted to the machinery that turned the spindles, reels, twisters, and all other equipment necessary for full operation.

Tom Anderton was one of the numerous families that had followed the Cherry Cotton Mill to Florence from Barton in Colbert County, Alabama. At Barton the cotton factory was known as Mountain Mills. The editor of The Weekly Enterprise of Sheffield visited this factory and mill town the year before the mill was dismantled and moved to East Florence. He gave an interesting account of this early forerunner of East Florence's Cherry Cotton Mill:

"The buildings are simply elegant and the machinery is of the latest style and embraces all the modern improvements for making cotton yarns. It works about 100 operators, mostly women and children. Its capacity is 600 spindles, consumes 1500 bales of cotton per year, and makes 2,000 pounds of yarn 21 per day with a payroll of $1500 per month. The products are sold almost exclusively in Philadelphia, New York and Providence, Rhode Island, which cities take all the products of the mill. The little city of Mountain Mills contains about 300 inhabitants and is cumbered among the hills two miles and half from the railroad. It has the appearance of being one of the most happy communities in the whole country, and while rather isolated from the balance of the world, you will find as much refinement and intelligence there as in any other part of Colbert County. It has a good union church and a good school building with no saloons, and no temples of justice as the citizens have no lawsuits or infractions of law. The mills are owned and operated by W. H. Cherry and Company and C. M. Brandon, the Superintendent and one of the members of the firm, understands his business." (The Weekly Enterprise, Sheffield, Alabama, July 16, 1892.)

The ancestor of Mountain Mills in Colbert County was The Globe Factory, or The Cypress Mills, on Cypress Creek near Florence. By 1860 there were three dams practically within sight of each other. They supplied power for two cotton mills (The Globe Cotton Factory) and a gristmill. All of these mills were burned by Colonel Florence M. Cornyn of the Union Army in 1863. The Cypress Mill that was rebuilt after the war by the heirs of James Martin. In 1889 all interests in this mill were sold and many of the workers moved to Mountain Mills near Barton. In 1893, this factory was relocated to Sweetwater as the Cherry Cotton Mill. Most of the workers moved with the mill and became the cadre for the expanding work force. These two mills, the Cypress Mills Company and the Mountain Mills Company, became the forerunner of one of the largest cotton factories to locate in East Florence during the 1887-1910 industrial periods. The forerunner of Cypress Mills was the Skipworth Mills at the same site on Cypress Creek as early as 1836. In fact, Magnolia Cole, a daughter of Franklin Pierce Johnson whose family had the very earliest connections with The Cypress Mills, told of an earlier mill at the same site going all the way back to the 1820's.

After relocating to East Florence, Colonel Noel Franklin Cherry, brother of W. H. Cherry, became the chief executive officer. Following him, a Yankee from Ellensville, New York, Nial Childs Elting, became President of Cherry Cotton Mill. Elting came to Florence in 1888 to establish, along with another New Yorker, Colonel Robert L. Bliss, the First National Bank. It is said that Elting had a cadre of financial backers from his hometown. He wasn't in Florence very long until he became the presiding officer of the bank, Cherry Cotton Mill, and 22 other businesses. He was also a heavy investor in numerous other local enterprises. He became very rich, and having no heirs, left most of his estate to his beloved First Presbyterian Church of Florence.

Nial C. Elting was a dapper little man, somewhat less than normal height, but nevertheless, made a commanding, if aloof, presence. Not even his closest associates dared to address him other than "Mr. Elting." He wore a neatly trimmed dark brown Vandyke beard, stiff linen collar, white linen shirt, and a four-in-one silk tie. Almost always he was dressed in a dark gray or blue pinstripe suit with black shoes and gaiters and a black derby hat.

Elting was one of the few East Florence investors who did not lose his fortune during the austere financial days that followed the Florence Boom. It was said that he was an excellent judge of character, and could size up loan applicants almost before they gathered enough courage to ask him for a loan at the bank. Only one man beat him, and, according to one of his associates at the bank, Elting never showed any emotion over this transaction, other than to report later that the account had been paid in full, with interest. It was believed that Elting took the loss out of his own pocket rather than see the bank suffer its consequences.

Mr. Elting drove a Cole touring car, but it was said that he never understood how its gears worked. Sometimes he drove several blocks in second gear without being aware of it. One time he got into his car, which was parked on the north side of Mobile Street, and released the clutch which caused it to surge forward over the curb and stopped just short of the bank. For many years, however, there were some who liked to point out a small fracture in the wall as the place where Mr. Elting's Cole automobile ran into the bank.

The Cypress Mills Located North West Of Florence In 1885, A Forerunner Of Cherry Cotton Mill.

The photograph of the Cypress Mill workers was taken about 1885, and with only a few exceptions, every employee in the photograph later moved to the Mountain Mills at Barton, Alabama, and, in 1893, relocated with the Cherry Cotton Mill to Sweetwater Creek.

Left to right: (front row, kneeling) Jim Hawshaw, Henry Hawshaw, Sanford Hendon, Dela Hendon, unknown, Anna Eliza Nichols, unknown, Will Rickard, Roscoe Johnson, Frank Tucker, unknown, unknown. (Second row) Fowler, Henry Redding, Franklin Pierce Johnson (Foreman), Sally Lindsey, unknown, unknown, unknown, Mary Rickard, Cinda Nichols, Mrs. Ann Redding, Mrs. Lula Holt, Mrs. Mary Teas, Kate Redding, unknown, Janie Lindsey, Miss Teas, Neely Holt, John Holt (Master Mechanic), Tom Hawshaw, Will Nichols. (Third row) unknown, Dave Hendon, Robert Martin (Mill Owner). (Top of photograph) Frank Rickard.

Cypress Creek Cotton Mill (c. 1880)

Colonel Noel Franklin Cherry who with his brother, W. H. Cherry, purchased the Mountain Mills at Barton, Alabama, and moved it to East Florence in 1893.

Cherry Cotton Mill about 1900

Cherry Cotton Mill(About 1930)

Ashcraft Cotton Mill

Interior Weaving Room: Ashcraft Cotton Mills, East Florence, Alabama c.1910

Ashcraft Cotton Mill

The Ashcraft Cotton Mill began as a family enterprise made up of four brothers, John T. , C. W. , Lee, Erister and Fletcher Ashcraft. Their father, Andrew J. Ashcraft, was also engaged in the business until his death in 1903.

The business began as the Florence Cotton Oil Company in the spring of 1898 when C. W. and Erister Ashcraft worked together in its establishment. The nearest mills were at Nashville, Memphis and Birmingham. Cottonseed was selling at $5.00 per ton, and as a result of this local cotton oil processing the price of cottonseed advanced over 500 percent for the area farmers. Some 50 to 75 people were employed during the first year of operation.

The Ashcraft Cotton Mill was formed in 1899 from the Florence Cotton Oil Company. When this cotton factory opened for business in July, 1900, there was quite a celebration with a big brass band and a large number of visiting dignitaries.

John Thomas Ashcraft was its chief executive officer. The Ashcrafts were a large family, and John was the oldest of eleven children. He was born in Clay County, Alabama, in 1859, the son of Andrew J. Ashcraft who had surrendered with Lee in Virginia at the close of the Civil War.

Andrew's father, Thomas Ashcraft, was a hero of the Indian Campaigns under Andrew Jackson. The first of the American Ashcrafts was John who came from England and settled in Anson County, North Carolina.

John Thomas Ashcraft, of the Ashcraft Cotton Mill, received a degree in engineering from Auburn University.

In his early life he was an educator, and, in fact, was interested in the promotion of education among young people as long as he lived. He moved to Florence in July, 1889, and was admitted to the Alabama Bar Association the following September.

Employees Picnic: Ashcraft Cotton Mills East, Florence, Alabama Circa 1920

John T. Ashcraft and his wife, Anna A. Hendrick, made their home at Florence in the Hawthorne-Ashcraft House, one of Florence's historic showplaces.

In 1912, C. W. Ashcraft was listed as President, with John T. holding the position of Vice President and Secretary. J. O. Finney was the Treasurer. The Board of Directors were: Lee Ashcraft, Fletcher Ashcraft, R. L. Glenn, J. J. Douglass and O. A. Robbins.

At the formation of the Ashcraft Cotton Mill its capital stock totaled $100,000. A company-owned village known as "Ashcraft" was provided for the employees. The mill was expanded to 3,000 spindles in 1903 requiring 250 employees. In 1927 the name was changed to "The Florence Cotton Mill". The local newspaper reported in 1936 that the average weekly wage was $15 for a 40-hour week. It also boasted that "The Florence Cotton Mill" was consuming 4,000 bales of locally grown cotton annually, and that the mill's products were being shipped throughout the United States and Canada. The Florence Cotton Mill ceased operation around the end of World War II.

The Broadus Mill

Another cotton factory known as the Broadus Mill existed somewhere in East Florence around the year 1895. This may have been the cotton mill located near the intersection of Wilson Dam Road and Veterans Drive. Evidence of the foundation and some rusting machinery could be seen at this site as late as the 1930's. Franklin Pierce Johnson, a supervisor at the Cherry Mill, kept a ledger indicating that he was also employed to inspect cotton yarns at the Ashcraft Mill and the Broadus Mill in addition to his work at the Cherry Mill.

Gardiner-Warring Knitting Company

The Gardiner-Warring knitting Company moved its operations from Utica, New York to the old baseball and circus grounds at East Florence in 1927. This came about as a result of a group of local business leaders who invested $100,000 in the building to lure this northern industry. Twenty-five-year-old Jewett T. Flagg came as its manager. He soon became its principal stockholder, which led to the changing of the firm's name to The J.T. Flagg Knitting Company. During the Great Depression years this was one of the few Florence industries that managed to keep its doors open. This popular company, as did so many other American industries, lost out to foreign competition following World War II and was forced to close its doors.

1927 Landmark

The Facilities Used In Earlier Times By The J.T. Flagg Knitting Mill

Jewett T. Flagg, and his wife, Charlotte, did many things for the community. They established a ballpark on Minnehaha Street for the youth of East Florence. They were largely responsible for the Muscle Shoals airport as a result of their personal friendship with Eddie Rickenbacker, who was President of Eastern Airlines at the time. In 1952, the Flaggs purchased the old El Reposo Sanitarium and presented it to the city as the Mitchell-Hollingsworth Annex to the Eliza Coffee Memorial Hospital.

(Photograph courtesy of Mrs. Joyce Ingrum)

Uniforms were the order of the day among the employees at Gardiner-Warring Knitting Mill. The women wore green with yellow collars and the men were dressed either in khaki or white shirts. Those identified in the photograph are: Peyton England (center in khaki), Pink Tucker, Bobby Warner, Lena Golightly and Carol Robinson.

The Traffic Circle

One of the lasting memories of Sweetwater during its thriving years is the traffic circle, which was the hub of its business and political life. This circle was at the strategic intersection of Royal Avenue and the Huntsville Road, and part of the main artery from the east into Florence. Facing, this circle, which eventually became an isle of grass in the center of a busy Intersection, were Hill's Service Station, Doc Phillips' Auto Repair, the old movie theater, Rube Martin's Store and the T. J. Phillips' General Merchandise Store. On the northeast side of the circle was the popular C. A. Sullivan Store. Originally, it was located on the south side of Huntsville Road, and later moved across the highway, to the corner where it has stood since the early 1900's. Charles A. Sullivan came to East Florence from Madison County in 1889 to accept a position with Milner's Drug Store on Court Street. In 1893 he opened a drug store in East Florence for Dr. James Burtwell, one of Florence's leading physicians. In 1896, he purchased the business and through a series of building programs and improvements, established the drug store in 1901 at the most advantageous corner in Sweetwater, facing the traffic circle from the northeast corner of Huntsville Road and Virginia Avenue. Sullivan also owned a livery stable in the area.

Wood Product Industries

The Florence Pump and Lumber Company was established at the corner of Marietta Street and Vulcan Avenue in 1893. It produced the old-fashioned hand pumps made of wood that were used for wells and cisterns. It also turned out all kinds of fine ornamental woodwork. Shipments were made by rail and barge to all parts of the country. The peak employment was 165 men in 1900. It was said that some six million feet of lumber annually was consumed in this operation. A gruesome tragedy occurred in the plant as a result of a practical joke. One of the employees was tricked into running backwards with a wheelbarrow. Not being able to see where he was going he backed into a large upright saw that literally cut his body in half, from his head to his feet. The Florence Pump and Lumber Company moved from Florence in the early 1 900s, at which time the Florence Stove Foundry was located in the building. However, by 1920 this company had ceased to exist.

Dr. A. B. Bellamy, who brought the Florence Wagon Works to East Florence in 1889, established the Bellamy Planning Mills on May 21, 1901. This company was located alongside Sweetwater Creek near Veterans Drive. It was later acquired by Lewellen and Robbins and was called the Acme Lumber Company. A. M. Lewellan had moved his family to Florence in a flatboat down the Tennessee River. William McDonald Richardson, who later established the Richardson Lumber Company on Tennessee Street, was the manager of the planning mills. During the 1918 influenza epidemic, the company operated three shifts a day producing coffins for the defense workers who were stricken by the disease at Wilson Dam and the nitrate plants in Colbert County. Large draft horses were kept in company-owned stables at the lumberyard. These animals pulled the great wagons that were used for transportation.

The Alabama Stave Company was built near the East Florence railroad tracks in 1897. It produced six million barrel staves a year. Eighty people were employed in the plant. Another 200 laborers were used in the forests to cut, prepare, and ship the wood to the mill.

The Big Stave Mill produced white oak staves used in whiskey barrels. There was also a Florence Stave Company located in the East Florence industrial section of town.

The W. E. Temple Lumber Company at East Tennessee Street advertised as a dealer in rough and dressed lumber. This enterprise was established about 1900 by William Epps Temple who had come to Florence from Virginia. His home was nearby. Later, the family moved to Poplar Street. William Temple built a number of beautiful buildings in Florence: the 1901 Courthouse, the 1904 First United Methodist Church (burned in 1920) and the Florence Post Office. The Temples moved to Hopewell, Virginia, in 1914.

Other lumber-based companies operating in Florence were: The W. E. Temple and Company Planning Mills and the Nichols Shingle Mills that had a daily output of 40,000 shingles a day.

The ACME Lumber Company (about 1920)

The Tennessee Valley Fertilizer Company

Lee Ashcraft established this industry in 1897. On its first day of operation eleven bags of fertilizer were produced by, Ashcraft and one helper. By 1904, nineteen different fertilizers were being produced totaling 15,000 tons a year.

IMC's oldest continuously operating fertilizer plant is located in East Florence. This facility is also Florence's oldest operating plant. It stems from the ante-bellum days when a flourmill was located at this site. This flourmill went into production in 1860, and for some reason was spared the torch of the invading Federal army during the terrible Civil War. Lee Ashcraft, a member of the well-known cotton mill family, acquired the 1860 three-story building in 1897. Ashcraft established the Florence Fertilizer Company, and in 1906 added a wooden building to the 1860 three-story building.

The Tennessee Valley Fertilizer Company established in 1897 by Lee Ashcraft.

IMC purchased the plant from Ashcraft in 1909. Fertilizer in those days was in a pulverized form and used primarily for cotton planting. Improved technology was added through the years, and in 1990 the Florence plant produced high grade fertilizer mixtures primarily for soybeans, cotton, corn, as well as for small grain and forage crops.

The company eventually was sold, to a national firm known as IMC, and in the 1980's it ranked as one of the largest fertilizer factories in the South.

Other Important East Florence Industries

East Florence could be considered as Florence's most successful industrial park venture. In addition to the large factories, such as the cotton mills, the wagon factory, and iron furnaces, numerous other businesses of various kinds were locating in the area. These included several stave mills, a fertilizer plant, wood pump works, pencil factory, soap manufacturing plant, wood shingle mill, canning plant, cottonseed oil processor, coal gas plant, ice plant, and a steam laundry. Even wooden dishes were produced in the area between the Ashcroft Cotton Mill and the Muscle Shoals Canal. A number of these plants were short-lived because of an economic slump in the 1880's. The coming of the Great Depression in 1929 had a staggering effect on the remaining businesses, and by the end of World War II the industrial life of East Florence that had generated generous dividends for the investors, and welcomed pay checks for its workers, was over. As the years passed the families of the original settlers moved to other places. Some of the moneyed men who had brought about the prosperous times lost everything they owned. One chief executive of the prime time of the boom period was later employed as a lumber checker.

The Florence Ice and Coal Company

The H. J. Moore and the Chapin Ice and Coal Company were combined in 1902 to form the Florence Ice and Coal Company. James F. Hall, Sr., who later was elected Mayor of Florence, was an early manager of this plant.

The water for the manufacturing of this product was pumped from a clear, cold, and gushing spring and purified prior to its being used in the large blocks of sparkling ice that went into the homes in Sweetwater.

Florence Steam Laundry

J. J. Veid established the Florence Steam Laundry on the opposite bank of Sweetwater Creek from the Florence Ice and Coal Company. Veid, a native of Newport, Kentucky, moved to Florence as a young man and was active in the laundry until the time of his death in 1935. In the earliest years most of the Florence Steam Laundry work was by hand, and horse-drawn delivery wagons were used to serve customers all over town. In later years modern machinery was installed and a fleet of trucks took over the delivery service. Frank Rickard was in charge of the washing room. On Saturday afternoons when the laundry was closed some of the boys in the community would take their weekly baths in the large washing machine. Leslie Hall, a long-time foreman at the Florence Steam Laundry, and Harry Harper, established a dry cleaning service at the rear of the laundry.

The Florence Gas and Light Company

The Florence Gas Light and Fuel Company operated west of the Florence Steam Laundry just off Huntsville Road. This plant, with its main office in Cincinnati, Ohio, organized its Florence plant in 1902, and went into production in March, 1903. The local plant manager was W. James Salter, who had been superintendent of the company's Covington, Kentucky plant. The best grade of Kentucky and Tennessee coal was used to produce around 75,000 cubic feet of gas a day at the local industry. This furnished the city all the necessary gas for lighting, heating, or for cooking purposes. The rates were listed at $2.00 per thousand cubic feet for lighting, and $4.50 per thousand cubic feet for heating or cooking. This company also carried a full line of Welsbach incandescent light appliances as well as a stock of gas stoves both for heating and cooking.

Located on East Hill during the booming days of the East Florence industrialization. Owned by James and Harriet Adair Kiddy, it was especially noted for "Aunt Harriet's" cooking. Harriet Adair Kiddy was reared on the large Kilgore Plantation near Greenville, South Carolina, where her father, William Adair, was employed as the plantation overseer.

The People of Sweetwater

Sweetwater merchant Thomas Jefferson Southern Railroad Agent (Herbert Hoover won the election!)

Success Stories from Sweetwater

Sweetwater folk have a way of keeping up with one another. They usually know who moved where, who married who, and what others are doing in the ways of living and working.

Some of their most exciting conversations have to do with the adventures of those who grew up on the banks of Sweetwater Creek, and, to use a colloquial term, "made good" in other places.

They make a partial if not total claim on certain local leaders. Former Florence Mayors James F. Hall, Ellie F. Martin, and Will Eastep either came from East Florence, or married an East Florence girl, or had such family ties that there are claims upon them. This likewise applied to former Mayor Howard Gamble of Sheffield and former President of the Florence City Council Steve Pierce, as well as former City Commissioners Clyde Bohannon and Alva Hall.

One or the number of business leaders who made East Florence proud is Buddy Killen of Nashville. He heads up that music city's biggest and best-known publishing company, Tree International. Songs in the Tree catalogue include: "Green Grass of Home", "King of the Road", "Make the World Go Away", and "Mamas Don't Let Your Babies Grow Up to Be Cowboys".

Buddy's family were business leaders in East Florence for more than twenty years. His father, Willie Killen, owned the popular Killen's Café near the railroad tracks and across from the Gardiner-Warring Knitting Mill. He also owned and operated an East Florence taxi service. A brother, Burt Killen, is one of Sweetwater's 1980 merchants. He owns and operates the House of vacuums which is located in the East Florence Historic District.

Other Sweetwater success stories include the careers of Lauderdale County's Sheriff, Billy Townsend, and Superintendent of Education, Dr. Osbie Linville. In the mid 1860's former, Governor, Robert Miller Patton, came from Sweetwater Creek.

Some of the Special People Who Lived in Sweetwater

Sanford Hendon was one of the original employees at Cypress Mills. He followed the mill relocation to Barton and then to Sweetwater. Aquila Hendon kept excellent records of the deaths and births in East Florence.

Sanford Hendon in his early years was said to have learned the ways of applying Indian herbs to bring about the healing of some illnesses.

Taylor Wylie, an early East Florence merchant. (The original Freewill Baptist Church is in background of this photograph.)

Pictured above is Franklin Pierce Johnson and his grandson, Louie Cole. Johnson was supervisor at the Cherry Cotton Mill, The Cypress Mills near Florence and the Mountain Mills near Barton. His father, James Blassingame Johnson, had been a supervisor at the Cypress Mills before the Civil War. Franklin Johnson moved to East Florence in 1893, and built two large houses near the Cherry Cotton Mill that stood as landmarks until the 1960's. He served as City Councilman representing East Florence, and was a representative of the Singer Sewing Machine Company for the area.

The Johnson Place

(left to right): Claude M. Cole, Louie Cole, Mrs. Magnolia Cole, Robert M. Johnson, Franklin P. Johnson, Freddie Lee Johnson, Mrs. Mary E. Johnson, Elliot Johnson, Lucy Lavania Johnson, Mrs. Martha Nichols Johnson and Roscoe Johnson.

East Florence War Hero Grady Leon Gamble on Sweetwater Avenue. He united with St. James Methodist church on May 9, 1941 and was lost at sea in The Battle of New Britain on Christmas Eve night December 24, 1943.

Mrs. Edna Golden

Mrs. Edna Golden, a charming lady who gave much of her time and energy in the preservation of the historic buildings in the Sweetwater Business District.

(left to right: Homer Rickard, Alta Bell Rickard Crockett, Frank Rickard, and Hunter Rickard.)

The Homer Rickard Grocery is fondly remembered by many old-timers who enjoy reminiscing about Sweetwater. A navy veteran of World War I, Rickard began his grocery career as a clerk and delivery boy at the W. H. Matthews Grocery.

According to Florence's historian and artist, John Morgan, "Homer considered Mr. Matthews to be second father, and loved him very much." Homer Rickard established his own grocery during the 1930's next door to the L. Lindsey Grocery.

His parents were James and Mary Frances Redding Rickard. His father came from Cypress Creek near Florence and was connected with the Sam Bounds, Senior, Family who owned Florence's historic landmark, "The Martin-Bounds Place" on Cypress Mill Road from 1886 until about 1970.

Homer Rickard's mother, Mary Frances Redding Rickard, was a daughter of Duncan M. and Tobitha Ann Adair Redding. During World War II, Rickard served as Air Raid Warden for East Florence. He mustered volunteers to patrol the streets to insure that lights were turned out in every home when the siren sounded. He also had a fleet of high school boys on bicycles who served as messengers between the watch posts.

Homer and Sexter Butler Rickard had three sons and one daughter: James, Thomas, Nathan and Dorothy (Holland). James "Dusty" Rickard was a popular sports figure at the Muscle Shoals for many years. At one time he owned Dusty Joe's Restaurant on East Tennessee Street.

"Dusty" Rickard and his children: James, Hilma Dean, Becky and Jim. At right is a friend and neighbor, Claud Gamble with his small son, Howard. (Dr. Howard Gamble, a Sheffield Dentist, is a former Colbert County, Alabama Commissioner and a former Mayor of Sheffield).

Thomas J. Phillips is shown at left with his wife, the former Hortense Calloway of West Point, Tennessee, and two of their sons and two of their oldest daughters. Their Victorian mansion, Terrace Heights, which is a part of the East Florence Historic District overlooks all of the Sweetwater business area. A former employee in the mansion remembered that all meals were served in a most formal style, and that two servants were required to wait upon the large dining table, one at each end of the room.

John D. Weeden, developer of Weeden Heights. He owned the vast Sweetwater Plantation from the early 1900's until his death about 1955.

Ed Crouch worked at Sweetwater for John and Jessie Weeden for more than 50 years, beginning in 1906. Crouch, who died in 1958, had many memories of the Weedens and his responsibilities around the farm. Among his recollections were that he always received union wages, and that the Weedens were, by far, the best employers he had ever had.

Elizabeth Weeden Minton, daughter of John D. and Jesse Weeden of Sweetwater. She was married to James Minton of Hannibal, Missouri. Elizabeth was an only child and as a young lady she taught Bible stories to the young children who lived near the Sweetwater Plantation. This was a very popular class, especially for the young boys. Not only was Elizabeth a beautiful young lady, she was an excellent Bible teacher as well. Elizabeth served cookies and tea to her students in a formal dining room of the mansion, using the finest of Governor's china and silver.

Jesse Price Family at their Sweetwater Avenue residence. (The Sweetwater Creek flowed through their back yard.)

Jesse and Inez Wilkes Price had thirteen children: Edgar, Raymond, Roy, Nellie May, Virta Aliene, Elmer, Mamie, Doris, Virginia, Mary, Louise, Billy, and Barbara Jean.

Leonard and Lucy Lindsey with their daughter, Mary Ellen (L. Lindsey a prominent East Florence Merchant.)

Leonard and Lucy Lindsey had nine children: Carmel, Carlos, Pauline, Lura, Nelson, Howard, Marvin, Claud, and Mary Ellen.

Mainline Alphine

Among the unforgettable personalities were a number of ex-slaves, Uncle Mose, Pompeii, and Mainline. Uncle Mose was born at the Sweetwater Plantation and farmed for the Wesley Carter family in the early 1900's. Pompeii poured moulds for dog irons in The Foundry. Mainline, whose real name was Richard Henry Alphine, was born before the Civil War on the Alphine Plantation in Mississippi. He came to Florence in 1918 to work on the Wilson Dam Project. Afterwards he made his home with the Web Staggs Family on Sweetwater Avenue. Mainline, who was 12 years old when the Civil War ended, had many stories about the horrors of that era.

The photograph shows Cecil Wilson standing at right. Next to him is his mother, Mrs. R. H. Wilson. Seated (left to right are Mrs. R. H. Wilson's parents, Mr. and Mrs. John O. Barnett, and Cecil Wilson's, daughter, Mrs. Fred Carter, and her son, Lance Lee Carter.

Warm summer days were always a time for outings alongside the cool and refreshing water of Sweetwater Creek.

Sweetwater Creek, prior to its being invaded by man and machinery, was said to have been one of nature's most beautiful streams as it flowed gently through the valley and into the Tennessee River.

Miss Howard Weeden of Huntsville, Alabama. Her brother, Colonel John D. Weeden, Sr., was married to Mattie Patton of the Sweetwater Plantation in Florence. Miss Howard's poems and delicate art work were recognized throughout the U.S. and in parts of Europe. Her paintings of former slaves include African-Americans who once lived and worked on the Sweetwater Plantation. One of her paintings, "The Old Boatman" is thought to have been a beloved slave named Rome whose job included rowing Governor Patton across the Tennessee River to see his tall corn growing on Patton Island. In her final lines of the poem that accompanied this painting, Miss Howard told how the old master "passed Heaven's gate, . . . and soon he'll call across the foam to Rome . . . loose your boat and come home."

The Reverend J. B. Bloss who served as pastor of the First Freewill Baptist Church from 1922 to 1931.

Sweetwater Wedding Picture

The Rev. George Wilkes and wife Betty Livingston Wilkes. Wilkes, an employee of the Florence Wagon factory, was also a Methodist Circuit Rider.

Homes of mill workers facing Minnehaha Street in East Florence. At the rear of these houses is Sweetwater Creek which flows from the Sweetwater Spring on the ante-bellum Sweetwater Plantation to the Tennessee River.

Nathan Homer Rickard who died in 1999 at the age of 74 years. Nathan was one of the original organizers of the Sweetwater Reunion. The other members of this original committee were: Jimmy Ray Stanfield, Becky Owens Nelson, Alphonse "Bitts" Nelson, Mary Rickard Hughes, Mary Butler Fields, Reba "Bits" Spann White, Betty Staggs McDonald, Clifford Patrick, and Delores Rickard Sims.

Clifford Wright

A World War II hero who was killed June 6, 1944, on the Normandy Beach during the initial assault against the German beachheads. Clifford grew up in Sweetwater and attended the public schools in Florence. He was married to Helan Cole whose father, Claud Cole, was seriously wounded in World War I.

Swimming in Sweetwater Creek was a summertime fun! The dams were home made, using logs, slabs and feed sacks.

Front row: One of the Browns who could swim like a fish, Jack Staggs, L. D. Staggs, Jr., Marvin Lindsey, Howard Lindsey, John Young, Walker Hunt, Tinze Liles. Back row: Howard Cole, Albert Gamble, Dink Redding, Tommy James, Tommy Cofield, Leck Gamble and Doc Wright.

Transportation to Bar Bar Park

The nearest swimming hole for the girls was at Bar Bar Park on Cypress Creek west of Florence. The transportation used in the photograph above was the L. D. Staggs Ford delivery truck. The lovely young bathers were: Geneva Phillips, Reba Staggs, Geneva Staggs, Thelma Stancel, Irene Staggs, an unknown lady, and Grace Willis.

There were five foot bridges over Sweetwater Creek connecting Sweetwater Avenue and Minnehaha Street. These well-built steel structures with wooden floors were erected by the Cherry Cotton Mill for their employees and as a public service to its neighbors.

These bridges were gathering places for the youth in the neighborhood, especially on warm Summer days.

Pictured above are Martha James and Sarah Carden standing on one of the foot bridges across Sweetwater Creek.

Early Patton school near Sweetwater Plantation Teacher Miss Myrtle White(right)

Florence Baseball Team

Front row center Otis "Red" Carter
Front row far right Roland Hall
Back row second from right Lincoln Hall

The young people in Sweetwater gather around Sweetwater Spring to welcome home Fred Crockett, a World War I hero who had just returned from the battlefields of Europe. (Crockett is standing on back row second from the right.)

Love and Marriage

Edgar and Hazel Price celebrated 64 years of marriage in 1989. Their courtship began in their very early years as he delivered the daily newspaper to the Weatherford family door.

The Rawleigh man was a popular figure in East Florence during the Depression. (Shown here is Oscar Jackson and his family alongside his Essex of the early 1930's. The small child in background is Betty Staggs.)

Funerals: A Time of Grief And Loss

The extended family characteristic that was so much a part of Sweetwater was always evident when a friend or neighbor passed away. It was a time when the entire community gathered to show love and unity. This funeral was at the original Freewill Baptist Church during the 1930's. The pallbearers were ladies of the Church.

The Sweetwater Big Game Hunters

Left to right Collins Richard, Lowell (Bud) Gambler, Dewey Lindsey, William C. "Jay" Carter

Although they called themselves the "Big Game Hunters," these gentlemen were always content to bring home a rabbit or two, and sometimes a gray squirrel if especially lucky.

Former U.S. Congressman Ronnie Flippo

In 1976, Ronnie Flippo, of Weeden Heights, was elected to represent the 5th District in the U. S. House of Representatives.

The Flippo family came to Weeden Heights soon after the 1902 flood destroyed the Eagle Factory Mill on Shoal Creek near Lawrenceburg, Tennessee. At the site of this mill is a lovely valley that is still known as Flippo Hollow.

L. D. Staggs, Jr. and wife Ruth.

There could not have been this story of Sweetwater without the untiring efforts of Lester Daniel Staggs, Junior.

His collection of rare photographs is invaluable. Yet, his most unique contribution was his personal knowledge of its history of a place and its people. This came from a deep and abiding love for the Sweetwater of his early days. L.D. Staggs, Jr. grew up in the valley, and at an early age he went to work for his father in the family grocery store. He delivered groceries to almost every family from Weeden Heights to Ashcraft Village.

L.D. was born October 7, 1918 to Lester Daniel Staggs, Senior and Carrie Wylie Staggs. His mother came from Mountain Mills with the Cherry Cotton Mills as a young girl. His father, a native of Wayne county, Tennessee, came to East Florence as a teenager with a widowed mother to support. L.D. Staggs, Jr. married Ruth Elizabeth Guyse.

Railroads &Streetcars

An L&N Railroad crew (about 1930). The tall man on the front row (sixth from the left) is Charlie Miller who made his home near the railroad in Sweetwater.

The Railroads

After the big fire at the Florence Passenger Station on South Court Street near the old Indian Mound in 1906, all railroad activities for Florence and Lauderdale County were conducted at East Florence. A major spur had been placed in 1888 to serve the new industry being located in East Florence. This industrial spur connected with the major trunk line that ran through Sheffield and Tuscumbia.

Relocation of what was to eventually become the Southern Railroad from Court Street to East Florence, added the second passenger and freight depot to Sweetwater. Earlier, in 1888, tracks had been completed from Columbia, Tennessee, to East Florence. This eventually became the well-known L&N Railroad that served the area until TVA closed its phosphate furnaces at the National Fertilizer Development Center south of the Tennessee River in 1976.

The Louisville and Nashville Railroad maintained both a passenger and freight depot in East Florence. The passenger depot was located south of the Huntsville Road and the freight offices were north of the road. A small passenger train, consisting of the engine, a passenger car, and a freight car, made the trip from Columbia, Tennessee, on a daily basis until the end of World War

II. Originally, after stopping at East Florence, it crossed the river and turned around at Tuscumbia for the trip back to Columbia. During the 1920's, a one-way trip from East Florence to Tuscumbia cost 25 cents. It was considered quite an adventure to enjoy the high ride over the Florence bridge to and from that lovely city known for its Big Spring. Train whistles, they say, were memorized by the people who lived at East Florence. They could tell by sounds which were the passenger trains and which were the freights. Some could even call out the engine number based upon the whistle.

The Reverend Seaborn A. Owen lived in a large house on the hill above the tracks, after his retirement from the North Alabama Conference of the United Methodist Church. In the days before his ministry he had operated the telegraph service for the railroad. The preacher loved to recall his railroad days, and would type out make-believe messages in Morse Code with his fingers to the passing trains.

John S. Myrick served as railroad agent in East Florence for almost a half century. His wife, Tellie Lindsey Myrick, was a well known and beloved school teacher in Florence and Lauderdale County. John and Tellie were devout members in the Central Baptist Church. Their first home was located on Sweetwater Avenue next door to the home of her father and mother, Caleb and Nancy Jane Gregg Lindsey. This ancestral home was later inherited by Tellie's brother, Robert Lindsey. Both Robert and Caleb Lindsey were cotton and corn farmers. In the early days, long before the coming of the industries, Sweetwater

Avenue was the major highway leading into Florence from Huntsville.

Paul Tucker was L&N agent about 1930. Tucker also operated Tucker's Cafe and Taxi Stand next to the L&N Depot. This frame building with its covered porch also served as the unofficial loading and unloading station for the streetcar. Passengers could count on the shelter during inclement weather. They also would sometimes purchase Tucker's excellent hamburgers, sandwiches and soup while waiting for the streetcar.

The absence of the passing trains and the switching of freight cars and the strange silence of the abandoned tracks are remindful of the East Florence that was and will never be again.

Engine number 4 which served Lock Six on the old Muscle Shoal Canal. The passenger car behind the engine was known as "The Black Maria." (photograph courtesy of the late Joshua N. Winn, III. Author and professor of English Literature.)

The Southern Railroad Depot was one of East Florence's busiest places. There were lovely flower gardens on the front grounds that were planted and cared for by the ticket and freight agents.

The Trolley

In 1902 streetcar lines were completed to connect Florence and East Florence with Sheffield and Tuscumbia, and, later, with the U.S. Nitrate Plant Number 2 on the Wilson Dam Reservation. This was the first interurban electric line in the South, and was the major means of transportation at the Shoals for a period of some thirty years.

The winter trolley car that ran on schedule between Sweetwater and Tuscumbia. The early summer cars were open-type which enabled the passengers a good breeze and sometimes "scary" views, especially when traveling over the upper deck of the old Florence Railroad Bridge. These electric trolleys are said to have been the most efficient transportation devices yet invented by man. They utilized water-powered electric energy and produced no damaging smog or waste gas to harm the environment.

The Trolley descend hill into East Florence (1920)

The photograph above shows a streetcar about 1904.

On a hot day in July 1904, the coming of the new streetcar to East Florence was a gala event. People were lined up in front of the drug store and were standing all over the traffic circle and on both sides of Huntsville Road to welcome the first car to arrive on the recently installed track. Among the dignitaries in the arriving streetcar were: J. W. Worthington, L. McIntyre, C. W. Ashcraft, H. H. Burt, George Morris, and Mr. Hutchins, Superintendent of Southern Railway. The streets were decorated with banners and flags. The streetcar became Sweetwater's door to the outside world. Earlier systems had been constructed in the three cities at the Muscle Shoals during the boom days of the late 1880's. One of these was a horse drawn streetcar that operated between the railroad depots in East Florence and the Baptist University at North Florence as early as 1890. At first the car was pulled by a small steam engine. However, the wooden tracks were too flimsy for the weight of the engine. Thus, strong workhorses were used to pull the car.

There were altogether 12 miles of tracks in the 1903 system that ran from Tuscumbia to East Florence. The corporation had the financial backing of J. W. Worthington of Sheffield who had secured help from Henry Parsons of New York and George Parsons of Maine. This arrangement with people from the Northeast is yet another clue that large sums of money from that part of the nation went into the industrial development of East Florence during the 1880's and 1890's. Probably the full story will never be known, in that records are almost nonexistent. J. W. Worthington, for instance, decreed in his will that all of his records be destroyed at his death.

The streetcar line to Florence crossed over the Tennessee River bridge and entered the city by way of Crest and Reeder Streets. Its journey to Sweetwater brought it by way of Nellie Avenue, and then south on Poplar Street to Tuscaloosa Street where it turned the sharp curve at Angel's Corner to proceed south on Cherry Street to finally intersect with Tennessee Street. From there it made its slow descent into Sweetwater over a special cut that followed the contours of Catholic Hill into the valley below. The car tracks ran behind the row of brick buildings that faced the south side of Huntsville Road, and turned onto Huntsville Road near the front of the L&N Depot. The covered porch of Tucker's Cafe near the L&N Depot was used as a loading and unloading station for the streetcars. From Tucker's Cafe it turned west on Huntsville Road and rejoined its main track that led around the side of Catholic Hill back to Florence.

The streetcar operated on an hourly basis. There were times, however, when it came and went more frequently. The fare from Sweetwater to either the State Normal School or downtown Florence was 5 cents. To cross the river into Sheffield was double that amount, and the fare to Tuscumbia was 15 cents.

The yellow and tan streetcars were procured from St. Louis, Missouri, and were comfortable. The winter cars were closed with windows. The summer cars, however, were open so that one could view the ground from the seats while in transit. This created for many a frightening experience while crossing the railroad bridge over the river.

After serving the area for over 28 years, the streetcar era was brought to an end at midnight on February 3, 1933. Thus, one of the most efficient and delightful city transportation systems was abandoned.

Where the People Shopped

Staggs Grocery

This area was nominated by The Florence Historical Board in 1974 and placed on the State Register in 1976.

The Business District

Downtown Sweetwater at the East Florence Bank in the late 1920's.

The South Side of the Huntsville Road in East Florence scene from the 1980's.

Another View in the East Florence Historic District

Downtown Sweetwater

This town within a town had just about everything the East Florence citizens needed, and trips to downtown Florence were made only occasionally. In addition to the trolley a large bus, called "the Jitney", because it cost a nickel to ride it, ran to the large Federal defense projects during World War I.

Downtown Sweetwater was literally around Thomas J. Phillips' front yard. His large Victorian home was at the top of a hill, known locally as "Billy Goat Hill", and from his front and side porches one could see the entire business district of East Florence. Phillips, who served at one time as a Lauderdale County Commissioner, was a native of Lexington where his brother was one of the leading merchants and planters. The Phillips family were the original owners of the large plantation located near the mouth of Blue Water Creek, known in later years as the Cunningham Plantation. Phillips was an early investor, as well as one of the original promoters of the industrial development in East Florence. His general merchandise store, located across the highway from the East Florence Drug Store, carried signs on its front that read, "Dry goods, notions, clothing, hats, boots, shoes, groceries, flour, salt, hay and corn."

During the 1897 flood, the Tennessee River overflowed by way of Sweetwater Creek, flooding all the stores and businesses.

This occurred again during World War I, but the water did not rise as high in the stores as during the 1897 deluge. It was reported, however, that J. J. Veid had to send a wagon to rescue the ladies employed at his laundry.

Clay Reynolds was one of East Florence's earliest merchants. According to newspaper clippings, Clay was born at Waterloo and moved to Florence as a young man to enter the grocery business at East Florence. This early store was in a frame building located approximately at the site of the later L. D. Staggs Grocery. Clay Reynolds was a son of Thomas H. Reynolds, an early postmaster at East Florence. Both Clay and Thomas Reynolds built homes on the hill behind the drug store. Clay Reynolds, it is said, kept 300 head of goats that could be seen grazing all over the hill, and, consequently, the hill became known as "Billy Goat Hill". Billy Goat Hill was one of seven hills in East Florence that carried identifying names: Cherry Hill, East Hill, Catholic Hill, Chestnut Hill,

Granberg Hill and Old Cotton Factory Hill. Mitchell Brothers, another East Florence grocery at about the same period as Clay Reynolds Grocery, occupied a handsome brick building on Huntsville Road.

Drug Stores

The first druggist in East Florence was located in the Theole Row, south of the stove foundry. In 1894 the large building that was to house the Charles A. Sullivan Drug Store was erected. This was the earliest recorded business to locate in the East Florence business district. Later, it became the Cromwell Drug Store. Colonel Henry Cromwell, the second generation of the Cromwell's who owned and operated the drug store, led the local National Guard unit into World War II and the Korean War.

The ice cream parlor in Cromwell's Drug Store, with its iron chairs and marble top tables, was the gathering place for young people on Sunday afternoons. One clerk disliked this part of his job and would mumble under his breath at every dip of ice cream, "If I ever meet the man who invented the soda fountain I'll hang him by his thumbs to the highest tree in Sweetwater."

Old timers say that the drug store was a favorite meeting place, and consequently filled the role as the community social center. "People in those days would dress up to go to Sweetwater", recalled one who in 1990 has passed the three score and ten mark. "Saturdays always were crowded, and often on Sunday afternoons the young folk would gather in for ice cream sodas at Colonel Cromwell's place of business."

Colonel Cromwell later purchased the downtown Milner

Drug Store and was operating it at the time of his death. The next druggist in East Florence was Leslie Hall. During the 1980's this same building housed the East Florence Drug store, which was owned and operated by John Landers. There was yet another drug store on the opposite side located in the building that was later to be known as the L. D. Staggs Grocery Store.

Colonel William Henry Cromwell, patriot, civic leader and East Florence businessman was the second generation of Cromwells to own and operate Sweetwater's popular W. H. Cromwell Drug Store, Colonel Cromwell organized Company F, l5lst Engineers of the Alabama National Guard and led it into World War II. During the Korean War he was Battalion Commander of the l5lst. The local national guard armory is named for two veterans: Sergeant M. C. Pickens and Colonel Cromwell. Following Cromwell's death in 1964, members of his old unit wrote in tribute: "He sweated with them in Louisiana, froze with them through two long years in Alaska, crossed the English Channel and went on with his men into France and Germany."

Colonel William Henry Cromwell

Other drug store workers remembered were: Alton Capshaw and Fred "Cubby" Carter.

The East Florence Drug Store in the 1940's

The Groceries and Meat Markets

As far as is known the earliest grocery business in East Florence was the H. M. Ramsey Store. Members of the, Franklin Pierce Johnson family, who moved with the Cherry Cotton Mill to East Florence from Barton, Alabama, remembered, as their wagon passed through on the way to their new home, that Ramsey's grocery store was located at the edge of a large cotton field.

Sweetwater's business district was divided by the railroad tracks. The section east of the tracks is thought to be older than the area that grew up around Thomas J. Phillips' home and general store. Houston M. Ramsey moved to Alabama from Georgia where he had been engaged in the general merchandise business for some 13 years. An Uncle, Johnson J. Ramsey, had moved to Belgreen, Alabama, and following his early death, two daughters and a son moved across the mountain and began working in the Mountain Mill near Barton. Thus, the Houston Ramsey family had connections with the Cherry Cotton Mill prior to its relocation to East Florence.

The H. M. Ramsey Grocery was located at a strategic place. It was across from the intersection of Sweetwater Avenue and Huntsville Road. Sweetwater Avenue was the original Huntsville Road, or the main highway leading out of Florence to the east. Sometime after 1826 a more direct route was made that forded Sweetwater Creek and proceeded up what was to become McKinley Hill on to the Four Mile Branch where the Old Huntsville Road now intersects with the new four-lane Florence Boulevard. Ramsey's Store was at the west side of Sweetwater Ford. Buggies and wagons, while crossing this ford, would stop in the center of the creek where the water would reach nearly to the top of the wheels. This allowed what was called "the tightening of the hub, spokes, and the metal rims".

Houston Montgomery Ramsey

Houston Ramsey was a soft spoken and kindly man, and well loved by the community. The story is told that upon arriving at the store during the worst of the Depression there was a police car parked out front. Upon entering he asked his son what was wrong. "We've been robbed during the night", came the response. "What did they steal?", he inquired. "Some dry beans and white meat", was the answer" "Why son," Ramsey admonished, "you shouldn't have called the police. Those people were not thieves. They were just hungry folks trying to find something to eat." Ramsey died at the age of 74 during the 1930's, leaving three sons and four daughters: J. Thomas Ramsey, Lawrence M. Ramsey, Odie H. Ramsey, Mrs. Frank D. Hill, Mrs. W. S. Eastep, Mrs. W. A. Watson and Mrs. W. E. Coleman.

Two sons, Odie and Lawrence, ran the business until the early 1950's when the business was purchased by William Calloway "Jay" Carter. Carter, along with Acie Lee Evans, Jr., had been employed for a number of years by Odie and Lawrence Ramsey. Jay Carter was one of the sons of John Henry and Annie Wheeler Blankenship Carter, and had been reared on his father's and grandfather's farm east of Florence. Jay Carter married Lorene Watson whose family came from Mountain Mill near Barton, Alabama. Following his ownership of the H. M. Ramsey Grocery, Carter was employed at the Wilson Food Store on East Hill.

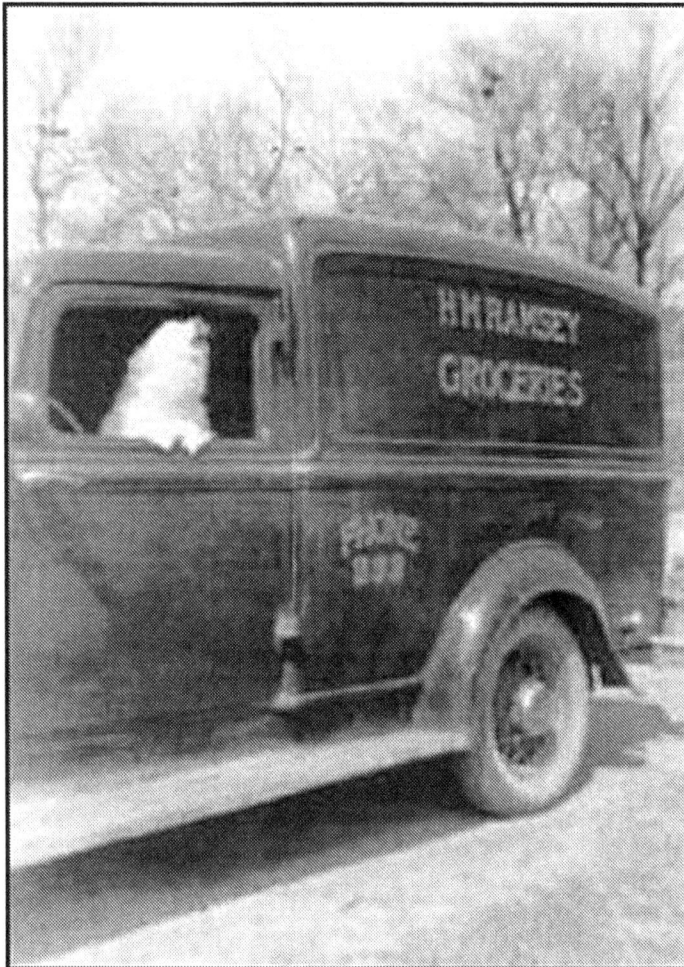

The Delivery Truck for H. M. Ramsey Grocery During the era prior to the coming of the big supermarkets, the delivery wagon or truck was an important part of the grocer's appeal to his customers. The customer would place an order by telephone or, perhaps, a hand- written note, and the grocer would fill the order and deliver the goods to his customer's back door and sometimes into the kitchen.

Odie Houston Ramsey was one of the most popular merchants in Sweetwater. When his father, H. M. Ramsey, died, Odie and his brother, Lawrence, operated the H. M. Grocery Store for many years. Odie was a member of the Florence City Board of Education. In 1960, he was awarded a gold pocket watch by the St. James United Methodist Church in appreciation of his fifty years service as Church Treasurer.

Mathews Grocery

William Marion Matthews opened his first W. M. Matthews Grocery next door to H. M. Ramsey Grocery in 1906. Matthews was a native of Lexington, Alabama, a graduate, as well as a former professor, at the State Normal College, now the University of North Alabama. One of the popular features of Matthews' Grocery was a "Mint Fountain." It mixed carbonated water with Coca-Cola, lemon, grape and orange juices. Extra large goblets sold for 4 cents, and a child's measure (4 ounces) could be purchased for one penny. Matthews later built a large two-story concrete block building on the east side of Sweetwater Creek at the intersection of Minnehaha Street and Huntsville Road.

It has been said that at one time or another every family in East Florence traded with W.H. Matthews Grocery. The late Irma Vareen Matthews Plott, of Rogersville, was a daughter of William H. and Laura Ann Robinett Matthews. She was an outstanding historian, and much of the early information about East Florence is attributed to her remarkable memory. Aubrey Matthews was a son of William H. and Laura Matthews. During his lifetime he became one of Florence's successful businessmen.

Behind the original store building was located the Horse Lot where horses were kept for the managers of the East Florence industry who usually rode in their buggies from their homes to their factories. Lester D. Staggs, Sr., was one of the early employees of the Horse Lot. The Florence Steam Laundry was later erected at this site.

William Morgan Matthews was born near the close of the Civil War at Lexington, Alabama. His wife, Laura Ann Robinett, came from Tennessee.

Matthews Grocery

Mr. & Mrs. Matthews , The Matthews Children: Irma Matthews, Plott, and Audrey Mathews

It has been said that Isaac Kreisman, opened his first store near the intersection of Railroad and Sweetwater Avenues. This was not long after he arrived at Florence via the L & N Railroad. He later located his Kreisman's Men's Furnishings at 101 North Court Street in downtown Florence.

The L. Lindsey Grocery

This immaculate grocery was an East Florence landmark until the late 1940's. Leonard Lindsey came to Florence from the Wright community near Waterloo about 1900. He married Lucy Lavinia Johnson, and, later went into the grocery business. At one time or another his five sons, Carlos, Nelson, Howard, Marvin and Claud, worked in the store. During the construction of Wilson Dam Lindsey's Grocery employed two delivery wagons. One wagon was pulled by a little sorrel called Charley and driven by Web Tucker. Lindsey later built a large brick and concrete block building adjoining this frame structure.

Lindsey's father was Adron Lindsey (veteran of the Civil War). Adron's father and mother were Phillip and Frances Sharp Lindsey of the Wright Community.

Phillip Lindsey's father, John, was an early settler of Cypress Inn, Tennessee. West of L. Lindsey's Grocery was the Big Nickel, a restaurant and taxi stand owned by Bill and Cecil Potts.

Homer Rickard Grocery

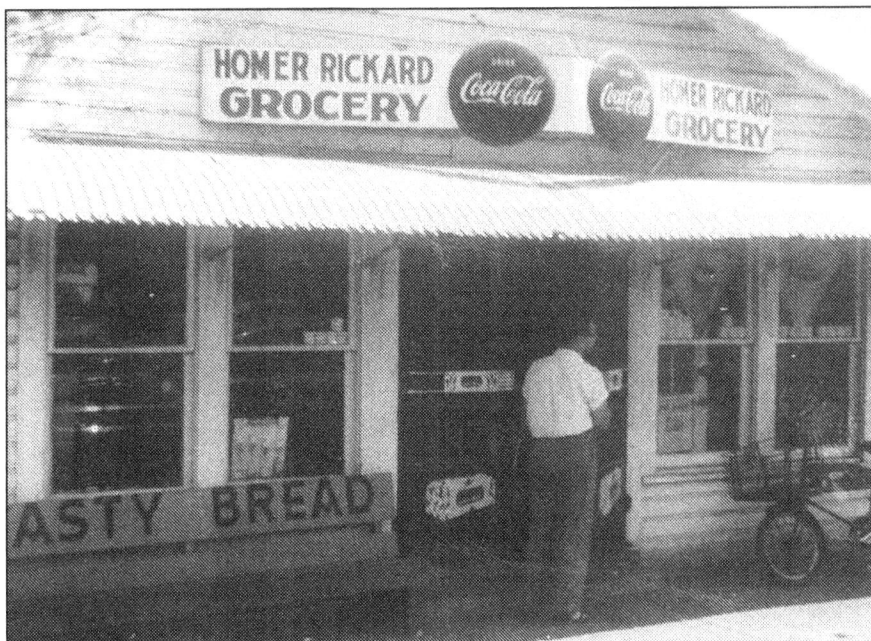

Homer Rickard Grocery on Huntsville Road with the delivery bicycle leaning against the wall. Homer Rickard and his three sons, James, Thomas and Nathan, operated this business.

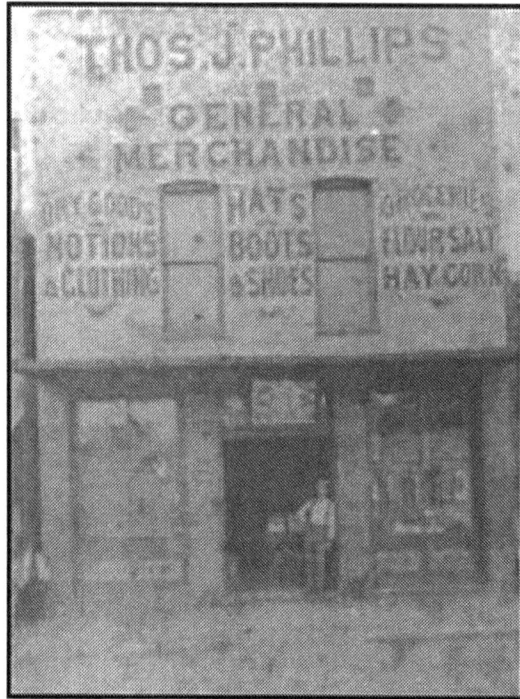

Thomas J. Phillips operated his large General
Merchandise on the opposite side of the busy traffic circle
from the drug store corner. Born in Lauderdale County
in 1857, his parents, Wilson and Nancy Trousdale
Phillips, were descended from early pioneers of the east
end of the county. The Phillips were the original owners of
the large plantation at Center Star that was later known
as the Cunningham Place. One of Thomas J. Phillips'
brothers, Andrew Lee Phillips, was a leading merchant at
Lexington, Alabama, for many years.

Phillips, a graduate of Chicago's Bryant and Stratton
Business College, was one of East Florence's leading
promoters. He invested in industry and real estate and for
a number of years was the East Florence banker. He

began his business career in 1890 when he returned from St. Louis where he was employed as a bookkeeper and went into business with two of his brothers. In 1896, he acquired full ownership of the General Merchandise, and expanded his interests into a number of other investments, including a partnership in THE FOUNDRY. He served as Alderman for the City of Florence a number of terms representing the Seventh Ward. At one time he was also a Lauderdale County Commissioner.

Thomas Phillips died in February 1933. His survivors included, in addition to his widow, three daughters and two sons: Mrs. Terry Howell, Mrs. S. D. Gray, Miss Martha Phillips, Alton Phillips and Harry Phillips.

Royal Avenue connects East and North Florence. Located due north on North Royal Avenue in 1990 is Glover's Plumbing Company. In earlier days E. M. Young's Shoe Shop was located near this site. Later, his son-in-law, Howard Darby, moved it to east of the traffic circle next door to the L. D. Staggs Grocery. North of Young's Shoe Shop was the early location of Florence's Salvation Army. This lot was considered at one time as a site for St. James United Methodist Church before it was located on Sweetwater Avenue and is now located on Cox Creek Parkway.

Photograph of an early delivery wagon around the turn of the century.

Original Wilson Food Center

R.H. Wilson Grocery

R. H. Wilson and A. A. Stutts opened their grocery store in 1921 at 218 South Royal Avenue. Later, Wilson, who had been a farmer, sold a wagon and harness and twenty-five bales of hay, to raise the $500 needed to buy out his partner's interest. A bill of sale dated December 19, 1934, showed that J. C. Phillips of East Florence, purchased a pound of steak for twenty-five cents and six bananas for ten cents. This successful operation expanded to a number of other Florence locations as Wilson's Food Centers, owned and operated in the 1980's by the descendants of R. H. Wilson.

The East Florence Piggly Wiggly

The first Piggly Wiggly at East Florence was located in the brick building across the highway from the East Florence Drug Store. Later it was relocated to the same side of the street as the drug store. Lawrence Ramsey, son of H. M. Ramsey who opened East Florence's first grocery, was the manager.

Staggs Grocery

Staggs Grocery is one of the few surviving East Florence businesses owned and operated by the same family who established it almost a century ago. It was first opened as the Taylor Wylie Meat Market. After a fire, Wylie's son-in-law, Lester D. Staggs, Sr., and a brother, Web Staggs, continued the business as a meat market and grocery. It later became the Staggs Grocery, with L. D. Staggs, Sr., proprietor. It is owned and operated as a cafe in 2002 by Lynn Staggs and his wife, Pat. Lynn is a grandson of L. D.Staggs, Sr. *(Previous photograph: Ruby Balentine Staggs, Billy Staggs, L. D. Staggs, Sr., Jimmy Holt, Doward Holt and Kenneth Brown)*

Picture of Model T Delivery Truck with Bill Hillis and Bob Watson, employees.

Jones & Wilson Grocery

In 1917 the Jones and Wilson Grocery was established across the highway from the East Florence Bank. Bill Jones had been a postman in Florence. The other proprietor, R. Gentry Wilson, had previously clerked in the Hennessee Grocery at Florence. Three delivery wagons were used during the Wilson Dam construction boom days, and the grocery expanded to two other locations. This business did not survive the Great Depression because credit had been extended to approximately 90 percent of their customers. Bill Jones returned to his former position with the post office and Gentry Wilson moved to Red Boiling Springs, Tennessee, where he managed a summer resort and hotel.

RAIN OR SHINE

Why Worry About Getting Your Groceries When You Can Get Them
Delivered Right to Your Kitchen At These Low Prices. Phone Us Today.

Sugar
10 lb.
48c

K. W.
Pole
BEANS
5c lb.

NO. 1 NEW
Potatoes, 10 lbs. 20c

WINESAP
Apples, doz. 12c

EXTRA LARGE
LEMONS, doz. 18c

1-LB. CARTON
TOMATOES 10c

GOOD
COFFEE, lb. 10c

CORN OR
Tomatoes, 2 for 15c

ARMOUR'S
Milk, 6 small, 3 tall 19c

QUART JAR
Salad Dressing 20c

Crackers, 2 lbs. 14c

TEA, ½-lb. 25c

NO. 2½ AVALON
PEACHES 15c

1000 SHEET
TISSUE 5c

LARGE UNWRAPPED
BIG BEN SOAP, 3 for 10c

BULK VINEGAR, bring your jug, gal. 19c

ANNIVERSARY
SOAP SALE
133 Years of Progress
COLGATE-PALMOLIVE-PEET CO.

PALMOLIVE .... 3 for 19c

SUPER SUDS, ... 2 for 19c
The Red Box for Washing Dishes

OCTAGON SOAP .... 5 for 19c

CHASE AND SANBORN
COFFEE, lb. 24c

ROYAL
GELATIN, each 5c

NAPKINS, 10c size 7½c

LARGE NO. 2½ CAN
Pork & Beans 10c

50-OZ. TOMATO OR GRAPEFRUIT
JUICE 20c

BANANAS, doz. 12c

BACON (sliced), lb. 20c

OLEO, 2 lbs. 25c

WHOLE TENDERIZED CURED
HAMS, lb. 25c

PURE LARD, 4 pounds 33c

FULL CREAM
CHEESE, lb. 17½c

BRANDED K. C.
STEAKS, lb. 25c

PORK
CHOPS
Small
Lean
20c

15c
Pound
Pure
PORK
SAUSAGE

Salt Meat — Streaked 15c
Fat Back 10c

Wholesale delivery Truck in East Florence

Lula Holt and her son, Cecil Holt, operated a small grocery store across from the Cherry Cotton Mill. The Holt family had been affiliated with the Cypress Mills in Florence and were among the families to relocate to Mountain Mills and, later, to Sweetwater Creek with the Cherry Mills. Lula Holt was a descendant of Caleb Lindsey, who was a native of the Wright Community, in West Lauderdale County.

Dudley Gamble and his wife Roxie were the next operators of the original Holt Grocery Store. Dudley Gamble was born at Mountain Mills. His family had moved to East Florence with the Cherry Cotton Mill in 1893. Late in life he moved to Cedar Town, Georgia where he died and is buried.

About half a block north was another grocery operated by Web Staggs, brother of L. D.Staggs,Sr. Joseph W. Pounders, owned a grocery at the intersection of Railroad and Sweetwater Avenue. He later moved this business to his residence, which was located near the intersection of Sweetwater Avenue and Branch Street. Other grocery businesses in East Florence were the Grimes Store, Turners Store and Goodwin's Grocery.

Cafes and Restaurants

Frank Rickard's Cafe was a popular loafing place during the Depression years. Those shown are (left to right): Henry "Peg" Grissom, Hobart Patterson, Ed Gray, Web Tucker, Joe Wheeler Brown, Charlie Miller, Percy Brewer, Buford Ramsey, Obie Tucker, Peaberry Coffee, Freebie Smith, Tom James, Red Walters and a Swinney.

Fulton's Cafe was a favorite place to hang out at all seasons. Those identified above are: (front row) Byrd, Tommy Cofield, Andrew Lindsey, Ted Lee, Hobert Lee. (back) Bus Staggs, Horace Staggs, Percy Staggs, Bob Wright, Fred Crockett and Bill Hillis.

Fulton's Cafe was probably the earliest Sweetwater restaurant. This small rustic building with a porch across the front was near the intersection of Sweetwater Avenue and Huntsville Road and close to the ford at Sweetwater Creek and the Huntsville Road. Before Fulton went into the restaurant business he had a meat market at this place.

A number of years later Jesse W. McDonald and son, Ervin, owned a restaurant directly across from the East Florence Bank. Later, M. B. Wallace operated the People's Cafe at this site.

Tommy Cofield, and, later, Frank Rickard had a cafe near the Cherry Cotton Mill. The building that housed this restaurant was an unusual structure in that it straddled a large ditch at the intersection of Sweetwater Avenue and Thompson Street. Later, Dudley Gamble operated a small grocery in this building.

When Gardiner-Warring Knitting Mill came to Florence a number of cafes opened nearby. One was owned by, Willie Killen. There was also, Will Porter's Cafe, Carl Gray's Cafe and Lucille's Cafe and Killen Café and Taxi Station.

Many of the mill hands ate their lunches, made of cheese and crackers or baloney and crackers, at the nearby groceries: Ramsey's, Lindsey's and Rickard's. Others would sometimes place an order for an R C Cola and a moon pie.

Tucker's Cafe was located near the L&N Depot and catered to train passengers and railroad crews. Plain hamburgers with plenty of meat, a spreading of mustard and a large onion, sold for five cents in 1939. A bowl of beef soup with two slices of loaf bread could be purchased for ten cents.

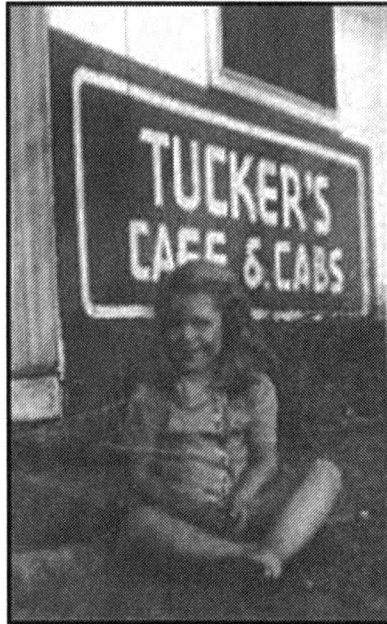

During the pre-World War II days Florence's future police chief, Noah H. Danley, was the manager of a cafe in the former bank: building near the East Florence Drug Store.

The Kiddy House

About the turn of the century East Florence had its own hotel, The Kiddy House. The proprietors were James and Harriet Adair. Its earliest location was at Aetna Street about a hundred yards south of the Central Baptist Church. Traveling salesmen, it was said, would go out of their way to stay there, because of Aunt Harriet's beaten biscuits for breakfast and buttermilk custards for supper. This establishment later moved to East Hill near Cole Street. The kitchen was in the cellar; a hand-operated dumb waiter was used to deliver food to the large dining room on the first floor.

Saloons and Houses of Prostitution

There were a number of saloons in East Florence. The earliest was the Spread Eagle Saloon owned by McMurray and Granbury, located near the intersection of Minnehaba Street and Huntsville Road. Another was in the main business section next door to Staggs Grocery Store. Until a few years ago bullet holes in the ceiling were reminders of some of the brawls that must have occurred at this place.

Although Sweetwater had its share of prostitutes, the most notorious houses for these ladies of the evening were near downtown Florence in a red light district called "South Seminary". The most infamous was Miss Kate. She was well funded, in that she was the mistress of one of Florence's leading citizens. An early telephone exchange operator enjoyed telling that almost every afternoon around 5 p.m. the wife of this merchant would ask her to ring Miss Kate's House. When Miss Kate answered, she was asked to tell Mr. Charles that his dinner was ready and to come home. It was said, that when Miss Kate died Mr. Charles gave her a beautiful funeral. One Florence historian commented years later "there were many mourners".

Theater

Around the turn of the century, East Florence had its own motion picture theater. It was located directly across from the East Florence Drug Store facing Royal Avenue on the west side of the traffic circle. This was before the talking picture show, and one sixteen millimeter projector was used so an intermission was held at each rewinding of the film. The seats were of wood that could be folded and stored. After the theater ceased to exist a small grocery was located on the first floor of this building. The upstairs was used for apartments.

Gas Stations and Auto Repairs

On the far side of the traffic circle across from the drug store was Hill's Woco Pep gasoline station. North on Royal Avenue stood the Oil Well service station. Near the Woco Pep station was an auto repair shop operated by Doc Phillips.

Hill Auto Company said to have been the second service station in Florence, faced the traffic circle from the southwest corner of Huntsville Road and Royal Avenue. Employees are shown in the previous early photograph. The mechanic on the far right is identified as Clarence Dison.

An inside view of the service station is shown below. Fred A. Hill, owner and manager, is standing at right. His father, Augustus Henry Hill is in the background. Augustus Henry Hill was born in Germany in 1844. He came to America at an early age and according to family stories, was the first plumber at Florence. At the time the City of Florence went bankrupt during the Depression, they owed him $2,700. He lost almost a whole block: of property including a house on Tennessee Street. Afterwards, Hill went into the barbering business with Rube Martin. According to family records, Hill and Martin became the first white barbers in the area. Augustus Hill died in 1942 at the age of 98 years.

The F. A. Hill family (shown inside the service station) are identified from left to right: Pauline Hill (Hillis), Charles Hill, Earl Hill, Estella Wilkes (Mrs. F. A.) Hill, William Hill, and Fred Hill.

Mrs. Estella Hill was a daughter of William Henry Wilkes. She grew up at Florence on Granbury Hill. Her family lived in an old hotel that had been converted into an apartment house. "When we lived there", she recalled, "we got water from Arnett spring. We had to go down a hill to the spring. I remember there were pine trees all the way down the hill. A lot of people went to the spring to do their laundry."

The Hill Auto Company had the Oakland Automobile dealership for the city (two of these early automobiles are on display in the previous photograph). A number of people in Florence purchased these cars from Hill, including Dr. L. F. Duckett, Tom Anderton and Mrs. T. G. Bryant. The Hill Auto Company later became Hill's Woca Pep Station. At one time Fred Hill operated the Hill Cab Company from this location.

The Pool Hall and A Barber and Shoe Shop

Todd Romine operated the East Florence Billiards in the main business district across the street form the drug store. It was later the pool hall of John Berry On the same side of the street was the Barbershop with its popular barbers, Baker, Nichols and Benton. On the east of Sweetwater, Jim Wess White, came to local fame as the barber who once cut the hair of Elvis Presley. North on Royal Avenue was Edward M. Young's Shoe Shop. Young's son-in-law, Howard Darby, later became its owner and moved the shop next door to Stagg's Grocery on the Old Huntsville Road.

The Radio Shop

The coming of the radio was a memorable event in Sweetwater. According to one source this novelty first came to East Hill in 1923. Homer Rickard brought a radio to Sweetwater Avenue, and the Rickard home was a popular gathering place every evening when Amos and Andy, and Lum and Abner came on the air. One resident of East Florence remembered that he could walk up Sweetwater Avenue during the 1930's and never miss a song on the local WLAY station's S.S.L. Hillbilly program. Every household was not only tuned in but had their radios at high volume. It was said that J. E. Winkleman and his son, Ben, sold these earliest radios.

The East Florence Bank

The East Florence Bank, with Thomas J. Phillips as President, was established during World War I. Newspaper advertisements show that this institution was paying four percent interest on savings in 1928.

The East Florence Beat

East Florence had its own police force. Actually, the patrolmen assigned to the East Florence Beat were from the Florence Police Department, but such assignments were on a long-term, almost a lifetime basis. A holding tank enabled them to temporally detain those arrested until they could later be transferred to the city jail. For over half a century these men performed their duties well, and a couple of them became legendary figures in tales repeated over the years. Most remembered were Will and Ben Romine, Ray Blakely and Bill Alvis. One story involved the conversation of two notorious drunks who had been arrested by Ben Romine the previous week. One challenged the other to go to East Florence and beat up Ben Romine. "Man", came the reply, "I may be drunk, but I ain't that drunk!"

The Circus Grounds

The large field between Sweetwater Avenue and the railroad tracks was known as the circus grounds. These shows would arrive by rail and pitch their large tents for the entire town to see. A calliope usually arrived with the circus and it would go all over Florence advertising the coming event. A lion escaped from one of these circuses and could be heard going up and down the L&N railroad bed for weeks until it was finally captured.

This was also the home field for the East Florence Baseball Team. Todd Romine was the star player in those days. The ever popular Dusty Rickard of the Florence Raiders started his career on this field. In, 1927 the Gardiner Warring Knitting Mill, which later was known as the J. T. Flagg Knitting Company, located its factory on this field.

The House of Vacuums is opened by Burt Killen in 1962, and was moved to it's current location in 1968. Six years ago the business was bought by Greg Davis. McAfee and Sons Sheet Metal Company was at one, time located next door.

The Wholesale Houses

There were two wholesale groceries in East Florence both on Huntsville road.

W. B. Simmons wholesale was located between the main railroad track lines in the same building that housed the 1990 Dig Store. The other was Bob Dabney's Wholesale Company at the intersection of Sweetwater Avenue and the Old Huntsville Road.

In earlier days, before Simmons and before Dabney, one eccentric personality would purchase boxcars loaded with bananas. He would wholesale these bananas from the railroad spur in the East Tennessee street vicinity. During the banana season he would walk all over East Florence and outlying areas with banana stalks on his back selling his fruit wholesale to the merchants. He became known as Banana Clark. It is said that upon being offered a ride by passing motorists Banana Clark would always refuse, preferring to walk under the weight of his heavy load. Clark's wife was Hannah Holmes Clark. It was quite evident to those who knew her that Hannah Clark was highly educated and had no doubt, at one time in her life, enjoyed both position and wealth. There is a bust of a beautiful lady in Pope's Tavern Museum at Florence which was presented by Hannah Clark and her husband not long before their deaths. It is said to be the bust of Hannah's ancestor, the Empress Carlotta Maximilian of Mexico who was the only daughter of King Leopold I of Belgium. The story of Banana and Hannah Clark is sad. They both died in poverty while living their last days at a small motel east of Killen, Alabama.

W. O. Goodwin owned grocery stores located at a number of places at different times. One of his earliest locations was in the brick building where the Central Baptist Church parking lot is located. This was originally known as Stafford's Grocery. It was demolished in 1957. Another location was in the two-story frame building at Weeden Heights occupied in later years by the L. V. Barnett Grocery. His last place of business was at the intersection of Kirkman Street and the Old Huntsville Road (now known as John's Market).

W. O. Goodwin and his wife had six children: Almon, Christine (Mrs. B. Edward Glover), Dorothy (Mrs. Robert Redding), Ruth (Mrs. Nathan Rickard), William and Jean.

Nick's Barber Shop

For almost four decades a young boy's first haircut at Nick's East Florence Barber Shop was similar to a rite-of-passage. In 1929, just as the Great Depression swept across the nation, G. C. Nichols opened his shop on the south side of the main business district in Sweetwater. Across the years others shared the business with Nick including Mr. Baker, Mr. Gilbert, and Tom Benton. This shop served as the "unofficial Sweetwater police Headquarters" for the East Florence Beat. Nick had a telephone and could easily locate Ben Romine or the other policemen more quickly than anyone else. Examination of old ledgers indicates that almost every family in East Florence at one time or another patronized Nick's shop. On September 16, 1958, Vito Cofield paid $1.00 for his haircut. Virgil Carter was charged $1.25 on April 7, 1961. An entry on October 26, 1963 showed that Hobert Butler's haircut cost $1.50. Nick retired in 1966, and one of Sweetwater's best known businesses became a lasting memory.

Schools and Churches

**The Maud Lindsay Free Kindergarten
A historical Shrine**

Brandon School

As factories moved into the new industrial section of Florence the people followed. A number of the mills erected company houses for their employees. Other workers who were financially able built private homes that, generally, were more accommodating, especially for the larger families.

It wasn't long before East Florence became a town within a town. People could walk to their places of employment, to their churches, and to the grocery stores, saloons, drug stores, dry good establishments, as well as to the local bank that had been conveniently placed in the center of the East Florence business complex.

Before 1893 the only thing lacking was a community school. Children who lived in East Florence had to walk all the

178

way to the Patton School southwest of the Florence Cemetery for their elementary education.

A movement was started during the early years of the 1890's to persuade the local school board to locate a school in the area. Charles M. Brandon, superintendent of the Cherry Cotton Mill, was the leader in this campaign. He was assisted and supported by the other two proprietors, Colonel N. F. Cherry and Nial C. Elting. Other active supporters for this community school were A. D. Bellamy and Jake Holliman, of the Florence Wagon Factory, W. H. Theole, of The Foundry, John T. Ashcraft, of the Ashcraft Cotton Mill, and Charles C. Chapin, owner of Chapin Ice Company.

The school was named for Charles M. Brandon (1859-1 898), superintendent of Cherry Cotton Mill. He had also been superintendent of the Mountain Mill near Barton before it moved to Sweetwater as the Cherry Mill. Brandon led the drive to establish a school in East Florence and gave the land for its use. It is believed that Charles Brandon's family was connected with the early Brandon Factory of Middle Cypress Creek.

Brandon School began as Florence's Sixth Ward School in 1893. It's first session was held in a dwelling house located between Richard and Patton Streets near the Old Huntsville

Road. Miss Ada Vandalia Coffee became Brandon Elementary School's first Principal. During weekdays while school was in session Miss Coffee used an apartment in this house as her living quarters. The other teacher at the Sixth Ward School during its formative years, was Miss Emma Hill of Florence.

The next session of the school, in 1894, was held in a large two story, brick building that had been erected as a commissary for the nearby iron furnaces. It was located at the corner of Aetna and Union Streets. The Sixth Ward School occupied the second floor and the Maud Lindsay Free Kindergarten used the first floor.

Two Florence schools were closed in 1895 due to the lack of funds. These were the Fifth Ward School located in North Florence and the Sixth Ward School at East Florence. Students and teachers were assigned once more to the Patton Elementary School.

When the Sixth Ward School was reopened Miss Coffee remained at Patton School where, as its principal, she became quite an institution for the next half a century. Ada Vandalia Coffee, daughter of Richard N. and Ada Crenshaw Coffee, was born in Lauderdale County, Alabama, in 1867. She died in 1949 and was buried in the Florence Cemetery.

Charles M. Brandon led the move to build The Sixth Ward School. He donated land for a permanent campus. A four story frame building was constructed facing Iron-side street and named The Brandon Elementary School.

No man had done more for the children of East Florence than Charles Brandon. He initiated a program at the Cherry Cotton Mill to promote the education of the children of the factory workers. This was before the days of free education, and tuition was required. The program was set up so that Brandon could see each child's report card. If a Cherry Mill worker's child received a satisfactory grade Brandon would, in turn, pay the student's tuition for the next session, which was calculated at $1.25 a month. In those days before child labor laws it was mandatory for the Cherry Cotton Mill worker who lived in a company-owned house to make his children available for work in the factory when they reached their twelfth birthday. Thus, Brandon's education program not only paid their expenses, it provided a means of keeping them in school as well.

Charles M. Brandon's parents were Washington M. and Mary Munn Brandon. Washington Brandon served as superintendent of the railroad bridge that crossed the Tennessee River at Florence. The Brandon family was active in Florence's First United Methodist Church. Charles Brandon was one of the organizers of the St. James United Methodist Church at East Florence. Charles Brandon died in Ashville, North Carolina in October, 1898 at the early age of 38 years. This was one year prior to the naming of Brandon School in recognition for his work in its establishment. Due to his health Brandon had gone to the mountains in hopes that the high altitude would improve his condition. His body was returned to Florence for burial in the Florence Cemetery.

The second principal of Brandon School was Calvin Price Anderson. He was appointed in 1900 and served through the 1903 session. Anderson was born in 1874 at Cloverdale in Lauderdale County, Alabama. Graduating with high honor from the State Normal College at Florence he had taught in both Lauderdale County and Madison County before coming to Brandon School.

Miss Mary Milner succeeded Calvin Anderson in 1904 and served as Brandon School's third principal for the next twenty years. After she retired as principal, Miss Mary remained on the faculty until her retirement in 1940. During this period she became very active in the establishment of the Brandon School Library, which at the time of her death contained more than 2,000 carefully selected books for children. This library was appropriately named the Mary Milner Library.

Miss Mary and her sister, Josephine, known affectionately as "Miss Josie", were probably the two most beloved teachers who have ever taught in the Florence School system.

Miss Josie was the first principal at the old Fifth Ward School in North Florence, and later taught in the Gilbert Elementary School for over twenty years. Mary and Josie were daughters of Florence druggist, Joseph Milner, and his wife, Margaret Woodall Milner. Joseph Milner's family came to Florence directly from Yorkshire, England, in 1848, to become associated with the Wood and Wren Woolen Factory on Cowpen Creek near Green Hill in Lauderdale County. The Joseph Milner Home stood for many years at the present site of the administrative office and chapel at Florence's First United Methodist Church facing Seminary Street. Miss Mary and Miss Josie were the last of their family to reside at this historic address.

During the period prior to World War I the Brandon School provided classes through grade five, which included the Maud Lindsay Free Kindergarten. Daily sessions commenced at 8:40 a.m. and continued until 3:15 p.m. An hour was allotted for the lunch break so that students could go home for the noon meal if they lived within walking distance. Prepared lunch at the school was made up of a bowl of soup and three crackers at a total cost of three cents.

The grading system consisted of four points: "E" was for excellent, "G" was good, "F" fair, and "P" was designated as a poor or failing grade for the student.

The demand for a larger and more modern facility became a pressing problem as the nation was preparing for entry into World War I. The two wings of the frame building were removed and the remaining structure was relocated to the back of the lot to make room for the new construction. The children were once more assigned to the Patton Elementary School during this period when work was underway. The large brick educational complex was completed in 1918 to house seven grades exclusive of the Maud Lindsay Free Kindergarten, which continued to operate as a separate institution.

The new school had all of the modern conveniences, including a furnace for central heating, indoor plumbing, and an excellent lunchroom. The year 1929 marked the beginning of the administration of, William A. Graham, an effective principal and a remarkable educator. No boy or girl who had gone to school under him would ever forget his influence. He built a school second to none in the excellence of teaching fundamentals. But even more importantly, W. A. Graham instilled a sense of moral value and personal worth to those who were fortunate enough to be at Brandon School. For a number of years Graham served as principal of both Brandon and Patton Schools. In 1956 he accepted the positions as Director of the Kilby Training School and College Supervisor of Elementary Student Teaching at Florence State College.

Former students remember Professor Graham as a giant of a man who strode across the hills of East Florence as he pointed the way to a better life through study and hard work. He represented the highest values, and stressed that manners and good behavior were the basic foundations on which to build for the future.

He died in 1989 and is buried in the Florence Cemetery.

Leo Creel, who had been serving as one of Florence's Associate Superintendents of Education, replaced Graham as principal. Creel served in this capacity until 1965 at which time he assumed another administrative position on the Florence City Board of Education.

Dempsey Rutherford replaced Leo Creel to become Brandon School's sixth principal. Under Rutherford's administration an entirely new educational center was erected. The 1918 brick building was removed, the adjoining streets were rerouted, and the crest of the hill was bulldozed and landscaped to make way for the new facilities. Robert E. Grice replaced Rutherford, as principal. The 1970 state-of-the-art Brandon School was designed in the "open classroom" concept to meet the requirements for a new generation who were destined to face the challenges of the Twenty First Century.

The Commissary Building at the intersection of Aetna and Union Streets was used for the 1894 session of the Sixth Ward School, which was later to be named the C. M. Brandon School. The Maud Lindsay Kindergarten used the first floor and the school was on the second floor.

C. M. BRANDON SCHOOL.

The two-story wooden school on Ironsides Street built about the beginning of the 20th century.

May Day Celebration in Front of The "The Old Building". This photograph was probably made during the 1930's when the earlier Brandon School building was in the rear of the 1918 brick facility. In those years the frame building was used as an annex to the new school and was referred to as "The Old Building."

Fifth Grade 1911 (First row) Edward N. James, Audrey McKinney, Clayton White, Mae Anderton, Annie Phillips and Katie Hewitt. (Second row) Salone White, Louie Cole, Odie Ramsey, Theo Wilkes, Jesse F. Eastep, Pink Gamble, and Albert Douglass. Miss Mary Milner, teacher, is not shown.

It was always considered a special privilege to be in Miss Mary's class. She was a kind and gentle soul and an outstanding teacher. Her life was such that every child wanted "to be like Miss Mary."

The Chapel (Brandon Elementary School in 1940)

Mrs. Mary Smyrl's 2nd Grade class at Brandon School in 1934

William Arthur Graham and the Brandon School Faculty

Front row: Lucille White, Koonce Riley, Elizabeth Garrett, Margaret Penny, Mrs. Neely, Frances Hafling, and Mrs. Plowden. Back row: Mrs. M. C. Dunn, Grace Paulk Young, Loretta Perryman Pittman, Elsie Duckett Dillard, Grace Smoot, William Arthur Graham, Katherine Orman, Cornelia Sloan, Bessie Ditto Trotman, Mary Milner, Lucille Wilson, Mary Douglass Bender, Mary Smyrl. (1942, Courtesy of Larry Davis Brooks)

Before Brandon School was established in 1893, and during intermittent periods afterwards, the R. M. Patton School served all the children east of Florence. This was the grandparent of the Florence City School System. A one-room brick building was erected here in 1847. The building was built about 1891 at a cost of $22,000.

In the early days one of Florence's wealthiest citizens, Dr. John R. Bedford, built his town house at this site.

The school was named for former Alabama Governor Robert Miller Patton (1809-1885). Patton had been a strong advocate for a city school system and had made financial contributions over a number of years.

One of the earliest teachers at Patton school, Mrs. Bettie Waters, had taught in the first one-room facility at this site. Miss Ada Coffee served as principal of Patton School for fifty years.

Patton School was phased out in 1960, and the building was demolished in 1963.

Long before there was a Patton School there was an antebellum plantation Patton School. It was located on Hough Road between the Sweetwater Plantation and the Wesley Carter Place. Photograph below was made about 1914. Myrtle White, teacher, is far right, back row. Third from right at back is Bessie Carter, fourth from right at back is Blanche Carter, and fifth is Lacy Carter.

The late Miss Dixie Finley, of the Finley Plantation on Hermitage Drive, remembered walking to this school as a young girl.

"I would walk from my house to the school over an old road-bed that had been used in the early days of Florence. This led through the Carter Place where I joined the Carter children and we would walk together across their pasture to the one room school. Lacy Carter was the oldest boy in our class and it was his job to make the fires the first thing in the morning. He would periodically bring in wood for the stove all during the daily sessions. Ben Fuqua's mother was our teacher at one time. It was a lovely place and I'll always treasure the memory."

This early County school was located on Hough Road near the antebellum Sweetwater Plantation.

Miss Maud McKnight Lindsay

The Maud Lindsay Free Kindergarten

The Story of Miss Maud Lindsay and her love for small children is one of East Florence's most beautiful stories.

The Maud Lindsay Free Kindergarten was founded on September 3, 1898 by Miss Loulie Jones in the home of Mrs. John R. Price. Assisting with the organization were Martha Brooks (Mrs. Frank) Jackson and Hortense

Calloway (Mrs. Thomas J.) Phillips. The Pioneer Free Kindergarten of Alabama Association was organized at this time with the Reverend Cullom Henry Booth elected as President. Booth was serving as the pastor of St. James Methodist Church in East Florence. Miss Margaret Cherry, of the Cherry Family who owned the Cherry Cotton Mill, became Vice President. Other officers elected were:

Miss Mary Milner, Corresponding Secretary, Mrs. Cliff Hallman, Financial Secretary, and Mrs. C. M. Watson, Secretary. Frank Jackson and Thomas J. Phillips were elected to the Board of Directors. The new association asked Miss Maud Lindsay to become the principal of the newly organized kindergarten on East Hill near the center of the industrial section of East Florence. The kindergarten became Miss Maud's life for the next 43 years, until her death on May 30, 1941. Miss Maud, as she was known by her students, made the children feel it was her privilege to, teach them. One of her earliest students, the late Mayor James F. Hall, Sr., of Florence, had memories that he liked to share about Miss Maud and his experiences in this learning institution. He almost always ended these stores by saying, "Miss Maud was a remarkable lady."

The original kindergarten was held in the bottom floor of the Sloss-Sheffield Furnace Commissary. The Sixth Ward School, which was to become the C. M. Brandon School, occupied the second floor. Later, the kindergarten acquired a frame house on Ironsides Street across from Brandon School. In the 1960's this historic shrine was relocated to the corner of Aetna Street and Union Avenue. It was moved again near the beginning of the first century and is located across from the entrance to Brandon Elementary School. Miss Maud's assistances in the kindergarten were Miss Ellie Houston, Miss Minna Scruggs and "Aunt Julia".

Miss Maud achieved national and international fame as a writer and storyteller. She was the author of fourteen children's books, and her stories were used in more than sixty textbooks and by publishing houses in Egypt, Mexico, India and South America.

Miss Maud wrote a creed, which became the foundation and cornerstone of her labor with children. It began with these words: "I believe that there is more good in the world than evil, more love than hatred, more beauty than ugliness". It ended with this affirmation of her faith: "I believe in the deathlessness of good, in the power of love— I believe in God, the Source of Love Everlasting."

Miss Maud & Her Free Kindergarten

Attending the kindergarten was a rare privilege. Not only did it serve the families of the workers in the mills and factories in East Florence, but children from other areas of Florence counted it an honor to be taught by Miss Maud. One former student from North Wood Avenue remembered catching the streetcar, along with others, at the corner of North Wood and Nellie Avenue and riding to the East Florence Depot where they would disembark and walk with Miss Maud to the kindergarten on the hill.

Another dimension of the story of Miss Maud's marvelous kindergarten at East Florence is that it continues to live and serve after more than a century at the same place and on the same hill.

Officers for the Maud Lindsay Free Kindergarten in 1990 were: Lavinia Tomlinson, President, Ila May, Vice President, Milly Wright, Secretary, Elizabeth Bowser, Treasurer, and Mary-Eliza Moore, United Way Representative. Trustees are: Mary Jo Carter, Virginia Bower and Ellie Mitchell.

This snapshot of the kindergarten was made in the 1950's before the building was moved in 1970 to its present location. The building has designated as an historic shrine by the City of Florence.

Religion

Religion came to East Florence with the workers. There was a common heritage among the Methodists, Baptists and Churches of Christ that went back to the Cypress Mills. James Martin and his partners had erected a union church for the mill workers. The Methodists and Baptists jointly used it for a number of years, and in 1878 were joined by a small congregation of the Christian Church, later to be known as the Church of Christ.

After many of the workers moved to Mountain Mills in Colbert County these three faiths continued to have services in a union church. A popular young Church of Christ minister visited the community more often than did the Baptist and Methodist and as a result a large number of young people joined that faith.

The original meeting house for the East Florence Church of Christ

Almost all the mill workers moved to East Florence in 1893 with the Cherry Cotton Mill. These people, along with the workers who had come with the Florence Wagon Works and the other industries, soon established places of worship.

The East Florence Church of Christ

The East Florence Church of Christ was located on the steep hill on Ironsides Street overlooking the Huntsville Road. It was later relocated to the foot of the hill alongside Huntsville Road.

East Florence Presbyterian Church

The East Florence Presbyterian Church was located on Enterprise Street south of Cole Street on East Hill. It had a large congregation at one time, but when the pump factory moved away its attendance dwindled, and the church was finally closed in 1923.

The Salvation Army

The Salvation Army was first located near the East Florence Drug Store on Royal Avenue. It later moved to Huntsville Road across from the Central Baptist Church.

St. Joseph Catholic Church

Sometime prior to 1898 the Saint Joseph Catholic Church was organized on Maxwell Hill overlooking the Florence Cemetery.

The earliest meeting place was in a small frame building on land donated by Mrs. Lena Peters. This area of Maxwell Hill became known as "Catholic Hill." The construction of a larger sanctuary began in 1898. Completed in 1902, it served the parish for the next seventy-five years. A new brick school was erected in 1948 with another addition completed in 1962. In 1959, a rectory and activities building were erected. The present Saint Joseph Catholic Church sanctuary was completed in 1974.

Faith Tabernacle

Faith Tabernacle one of the areas largest congregations was organized about 1936 on Cherry Hill. Its first pastor was the Reverend Cicero P. Melton. In 1937 the congregation built a small 25 feet by 30 feet frame church at 1225 Iowa Street on Cherry Hill. In 1959 a larger structure (measuring 30 by 60 feet) was erected nearby on Thompson Street. In May 1983 Faith Tabernacle under the leadership of the Reverend Henry Melton, a son of its first pastor, was relocated to Florence Boulevard east of Florence.

(This African-American baptism was a familiar scene during the early days in Sweetwater.)

Church of the Nazarene

The Above Picture is the congregation of the First Church of the Nazarene about 1940. This church was originally located at the foot of Tennessee Cut on North Royal Avenue.

First Free Will Baptist Church

Shown above is the original First Freewill Baptist Church which was organized January 17, 1904 and the church constructed in the spring of that year. Will C. Dowdy served as Clerk with G. W. Mitchell Moderator. Other leaders of this early congregation were: W. G. Watson, G. B. Kilburn, Call Lindsey, John W. Holt, Francis Marion Teas (veteran of the Civil War), M. A. Holt, A. Mitchell, A. Holt, Surantha Scott, Eter Holt, , Janie Lindsey, A. H. Kilburn, A. B. Waldrop, M. J. Waldrop, S. G. Shade and Ludie Riley.

View of the original First Freewill Baptist Church erected in 1904 at the intersection of Sweetwater Avenue and Branch Street.

The church was relocated in 1944 to the corner of Sweetwater Avenue and Stevenson street. In 1964, the new facilities were constructed at 1701 Florence Boulevard. It is now one of the leading congregations of Florence.

First Freewill Baptist Church, 1950

The second Church site was located near the intersection of Sweetwater Avenue and Huntsville Road. This photograph was made about 1950. Later the church moved to Florence Boulevard.

St. James United Methodist Church

St. James United Methodist Church was located beside a small spring on Sweetwater Creek near the Cherry Cotton Mill. Prominent leaders in the cotton mill and wagon factory were instrumental in the founding of this church. In fact, the name St. James was suggested by Miss Emma Cherry, because, she said, the book of, James was her favorite of the New Testament. Emma Cherry was a sister to Colonel N. F. Cherry of the Cherry Cotton Mill.

This original frame building served the St. James United Methodist Church at Sweetwater Avenue in East Florence from 1895 until 1927. It was built by the Cherry brothers in Mountain Mills near Barton, Alabama, as a union church for the mill workers at a cost of $900. After Cherry Cotton Mill was moved to Sweetwater, this building was dismantled in 1895 and shipped by rail to East Florence at a cost of $300. It was reassembled on Sweetwater Avenue by the Methodists. The ladies of St. James raised the first $100 for the cost of moving this lovely sanctuary. It was torn down in 1927 to make way for a larger St. James (which was destroyed by fire during the early years of World War II).

In 1989 St. James was relocated to the new Cox Creek Parkway.

Outings and Picnics

A Summer Outing for the Boys Class at the First Freewill Baptist Church. Sweetwater Creek flowed alongside Branch Street near the original meeting house. James and Charles McDonald are shown third and fourth from the right. Their father, Aphonse McDonald, was Superintendent of the Sunday School for fifty years.

St. James United Methodist Church gathers at Cypress Creek for annual picnic on July 15, 1922. <u>First row:</u> Lunette Lewis, Edward Lewis, Ruby Lewis Dial, Mrs. B. F. Richardson, Abner Richardson, Sally Tucker, Freddie Watson, Susie Gamble, Sherman Staggs, Louise McDonald, Annie W. Carter, Mrs. W. E. Watson, Mrs. Claud Carter (holding Fred, Jr.), Una White Reeder, Mrs. Hal Vessell, Lucy Gamble, Mrs. W. A. Kennedy, Mrs. Felix White, Dora Ramsey Hill, Mrs. Odie Ramsey (holding Ruby Dean), Lowell Gamble, Minnie Kerby, Hattie Freeman (and baby), Ethel Hardeman, Jackie Fields, Mary Richardson, Gladys Redding Roberts, (lady and child), Effie Johnson, Mrs. R. R. Boyles, Frank Carter, Thompse Redding, (lady in chair unknown), Elsie Fields, Mr. Grissom, Otis White, Dave Brown (holding Joyce), Mrs. Dave Brown, Henry Carter, Mrs. Gray, Minnie Carter Harris (holding Glenn), Mrs. Hornbuckle,

Center row: Freeman, Virginia Brown, Everett Gamble, Lura Lindsey Hall, Willodean Watson, unknown, unknown, Rhoda Redding, Grimes, Hornbuckle, Edith Hill Chard, Helen Carter Danley (holding Lillian Kennedy), Lucille Adams Ryan, White, White, Kerby, Kerby.

Top row: Valton Vessell, W. C. Carter, Isaac Redding, Cecil Ramsey, Lacy Carter, Charles Hill, Elsie Carter, Thora Hall Carter, Valeria Hardeman, Shultz Boston, Mazie Ramsey Coleman, Hornbuckle, Arline White, Emma Lee Boyles, O. L. Carter, Minnie Ray, Annie Pearl Kerby, Lila Terrell, Howard Redding, Mary Williams, Irby Pounders, Aubrey Richardson unknown child, Pauline Kerby, Pauline Lindsey McDonald, Alice Boyles, Irene Kirby Marks, Lincoln Hall, Ora Gamble McPeters, Ella Carter James, Mrs. J. O. Hall (wife of minister), Mattie Carter, Frank Hill, Paul Gamble, F. E. Gamble, Fred Carter, Sr. (courtesy Mrs. Ruby Dean Friar).

The Wesley Carter Men's Bible Class about 1930.

Those identified in the class are: Hale, John Hall, Walter Mason, Frank Hill, Henry Carter, E. M. Young, Marvin Kennedy, William C. "Jay" Carter, Otis Carter, John Gamble, Elizabeth Gamble, Frank Carter, Henry Bourland, Paul Gamble, William Wesley Carter, Everette Gamble, Dudley Gamble, E. Mercer Edwards, James Beadle, Houston M. Ramsey, Rome Rickard, Virgil Carter, Leonard Lindsey and Lowell Gamble.

Central Baptist Church

The Central Baptist Church was established as a mission by the First Baptist Church of Florence on March 4, 1900. There were a number of influential men who worked in this mission, including Dr. A. D. Bellamy, the first president of the Florence Wagon Factory, John T. Ashcraft and his brother, Cyrus, who were executives at the Ashcraft Cotton Mill. The first meeting place was at the corner of Central Avenue and Aetna Streets. In 1919, the name was changed from East Florence Baptist Church to Central Baptist Church because of its location on Central Avenue.

The Men's Bible Class in the 1950's

Summer Time Revivals

Revivals were known, not only for their religious significance, but for their social function as well. Summer revivals were looked forward to among all of the churches in East Florence as the highlight of the year. The above photograph was taken in July 1926 at the Central Baptist Church.

Central Baptist Church Picnic

This summer picnic, probably about 1922, was held near the home of Tellie and John Myrick on Sweetwater Avenue. This park-like area was near the cool and refreshing waters of Sweetwater Creek.

The Baptizing Hole

Modern facilities inside the Twentieth Century Church have all but eliminated the old summer scenes where the congregation met at the creeks for the sacred ritual. These photographs were made at the pumping station on Cypress Creek. Earlier baptisms in East Florence were almost always held at one of the two baptizing holes on Sweetwater Creek. One was near the very earliest location of the Freewell Baptist Church at Sweetwater Avenue and Branch Street. The other was close to the Cherry Cotton Mill.

The free flowing waters at both Sweetwater and Cypress Creeks were cold, even in the hottest days of summer. On one occasion a visitor from Turkey witnessed a baptism near Florence and later inquired of a teacher at Coffee High School, "Why did those people walk into the water all dressed in their best clothes?"

Weeden Heights and the Weeden School

Weeden Heights

Weeden Heights is one of the areas of East Florence. It was carved from the lands of one of the Tennessee Valley's great ante-bellum plantations, Sweetwater. This plantation at the head of Sweetwater Creek, and a large tract of land by the same name at the mouth of Sweetwater Creek, became the genesis of an entire area east of Florence that became known as Sweetwater.

John Downing Weeden, grandson of former Alabama Governor Robert Miller Patton, came to Florence from Huntsville in 1904 and opened the J. D. Weeden Real Estate Company. A number of years later he purchased his ancestral plantation, Sweetwater, from the other heirs. This lovely Georgian mansion, with its 3,800 acres of fields and forests, became the home of John and his wife, Jessie Earthman Weeden, for the remaining years of their lives. Their only child, Elizabeth, lived on the plantation until she became the wife of James W. Minton and moved to Hannibal, Missouri.

World War I brought about many changes in the small and rural communities of Florence, Sheffield and Tuscumbia. Approximately $82 million was funneled into the construction of two nitrate plants in Colbert County, plus an additional $47 million over the next seven years in the construction of Wilson Dam.

Weeden Heights and its neighbor, Pine Ridge, were born during the World War I and Wilson Dam boom years. Both subdivisions were sold from the Sweetwater plantation, which lands at one time included the site of the Tennessee Valley Authority Reservation on the north bank of Wilson Dam.

There were three small 40-acre farms located within these two subdivisions that Governor Patton had willed to his former slaves at Sweetwater.

A small business district at Weeden Heights evolved over a period of time. John D. Weeden gave land for the school in the area that bears his name, and a number of churches were located nearby.

Old-timers remember that one of the first airplanes to fly over the Florence Wagon Factory landed in a field near the present Weeden Heights community.

On Sunday, December 14, 1941, at 3:30 p.m a few days following the bombing of Pearl Harbor, a U.S. Army tri-motored Hudson bomber crashed in Weeden Heights, killing its two officers: Lieutenant James William Riddell of Moorhead, Mississippi, and Lieutenant Norris W. Brown of Hastings, Nebraska, The flight originated in Long Beach, California and its destination was classified as secret. The two officers were burned beyond recognition.

Weeden Heights became the home of a number of prominent citizens whose descendants would become leaders in both the business world as well as state and national governments. Among these was the Flippo family who came from Flippo Hollow on Shoal Creek near Lawrenceburg, Tennessee. They had been with the Eagle Factory Mill at that place until it was washed away by high waters in 1902. One of the unusual businesses to be organized at Weeden Heights in East Florence was the Pride Of Dixie Syrup Company. It not only survived the Great Depression, it exists in the 1990's as a regional and national producer and distributor of syrup. W. L. Craft came to Weeden Heights in the 1920's from Athens, Alabama, and opened a grocery in the old McCluskey building. At the rear of this store he began making candy in an abandoned tin barn. In 1927 he switched from candy to syrup, and thus was born a nationally recognized product Pride Of Dixie Syrup. A number of former employees of this company who remember their association with Craft are: Roy and Edsel Hunt and James and Ed Fenn. They recall that Craft had three sons and a daughter: W. L., Jr., Hollis, Griffen and Katherine. Craft placed his daughter Katherine's picture on the famous label that appears on all the syrup cans distributed. The Pride Of Dixie Syrup Company moved many years ago to Sheffield, Alabama, and Bono, Arkansas, and is identified as a national syrup producer.

Pride of Dixie Syrup a 20th Century national syrup company that saw its beginnings at Weeden Heights in East Florence

Weeden Heights early water supply came from the nearby Sweetwater Plantation.

There were two hydraulic rams in Sweetwater Spring below this mansion. One was used to serve the plantation. The other was connected with a large water tank that served the homes in Weeden Heights. Cost for this water was at a rate of $1.00 a month. J. B. Dobson installed the rams and Homer Dooley was employed by the Weedens to maintain the system.

Ed Crouch worked at Sweetwater for John and Jessie Weeden for more than 50 years, beginning in 1906. Crouch, who died in 1958, had many memories of the Weedens and his responsibilities around the farm. He spoke of the Weedens as being, the best employers he had ever had.

John D. Weeden on horse talking to one of the tenants on the Sweetwater Plantation (about 1919).

Sweetwater also had a dairy, owned and operated by John D. Weeden as part of the Plantation.

Herschel Rickard worked his way through school as a milk hand at this dairy. He would began his chores at 3 a.m.

so as to be in school at 8 a.m. One night he walked in his sleep and milked all the cows without the benefit of a bucket. He didn't discover this misfortune until he reported that morning at 3 a.m. to begin milking the cows.

The land for Weeden School was given by John D. Weeden during the Wilson Dam Boom days of the early 1920's as part of his Weeden Heights development project. It became the third educational center in the area promoted by the Weeden and Patton Families of the Sweetwater Plantation.

The above photograph was made in the early 1940's. This structure has been replaced by a modern facility. In 1990, under Mrs. Kay Rickard Staggs Principal, this school became one of the area's most modern centers for learning and is rated among the top in its standard of excellency. Originally a part of the county system, it was brought into the Florence School System in the 1950's.

The above photograph is believed to be the sixth and seventh grades at Weeden School in October 1935. Those identified are: (front) Howard Littleton, unknown, Marjorie Cochran, unknown, Dorothy Goodwin, unknown, Mildred England, Ruby Grigsby, Nadine Guyse and Hattie Mae Jackson (small child is Jean Goodwin.)

(second row) Robert Hendrix, Samuel Holt, Edsel Hunt, unknown, unknown, Mrs. Wilson, teacher, and Julia Dooley. (third row) unknown, Marson McMurtrey, Leroy Glover, Eldon Thornton, Andrew Ferguson, unknown. (top row) Manual Harris, Aaron Wylie, unknown, Bertha Harris. Edna Matthews, Nadine Harris and Gladys Russell.

Weeden Elementary And Junior High School

The above photograph is the 1935 Class of the eighth and ninth grades, with A. A. Matthews, Principal. Those in the group are identified as follows: (First row) Lovie Faulkner, Mary Wylie, Christine Goodwin, Jean Goodwin, Nella Mae Wylie, Helen Hale, Lucile Johnson. (Second row) Mae Matthews, Ruth Guyse, Wylodean Wylie, Evelyn Guyse, Lucile Crunk, Helen Guyse, A. A. Matthews, unknown, Graham Elam. (Third row) Malcolm Fenn, Edward "Pete" Glover, Lillie Mae Wylie, Mary Johnson.

Barnetts Grocery, Weeden Heights' oldest store building, has housed a number of merchants over the years: McClure's Store, W.O. Goodwin's Grocery, Bill and Auvin McKee's Grocery and C. V. Beasley's Grocery.

It was the original meeting place, prior to 1927, for the Weeden Heights United Methodist Church.

A New Beginning

Camera Crews Film the 1990 Sweetwater Reunion

A Silent Reminder of What Once Was

There is a strange silence now in East Florence. A number of conditions led to the demise of the factories and, lastly, the business district. Except for a couple of surviving companies, the industries that breathed life into the community have faded with time. The Great Depression and foreign competition, especially in the cotton and clothing business, sealed the final chapter in its troubled economy. All but a few of the workers have long since departed. Their children and their children's children have moved away to seek the new challenges of a more complicated high-technology society. History will record that East Florence thrived as an industrial section of town, and as a city within a city, for almost half a century. It was self-supporting. Its workers could walk to their jobs, to church, store, school, and to just about anywhere it was important or necessary for them to go. This feature, more than anything else, was what made East Florence a unique and successful experiment as a combination industrial park, business district and subdivision.

Sweetwater was more than a place on the map. For those who lived and worked there it became a community with strong ties. Its citizens and their descendants developed a strong and abiding sense of commitment and loyalty, to a life that was wonderful and to a community that will be remembered forever.

New Patton Island Bridge Gateway to Florence by way of East Florence.

The new Patton Island Bridge under construction in 2002.

The new entrance into Florence by way of the Patton Island Bridge will bring a new challenge and a new beginning to Sweetwater, which will become the new gateway into the City from al directions north, south, east, and west.

A New Beginning

With the completion of the 21-century Patton Island Bridge the new entrance into Florence will be by way of East Florence. Thus, a new beginning in expected to bring new life into a section of Florence that will forever be remembered as Sweetwater.

Index

232

H

Hafling
Frances, 192

Hale, 213
Brandon, 59
Claborrn, 59
Helen, 226

Hall
Alva, 94
J. O., 212
James F., 89, 94
James F., Sr., 89, 196
John, 213
Leslie, 90, 142
Lincoln, 120, 212
Lura Lindsey, 212
Roland, 120

Hallman
Cliff, 196
Clifford, 59
J. M., 65

Halls, 59

Hardeman
Ethel, 211
Valeria, 212

Hardiman
Stanley, 59
William, 59

Harlan
Sam C., 68
Samuel, 59

Harper
Harry, 91

Harris
Bertha, 225
Manual, 225
Minnie Carter, 211
Nadine, 225

Hawkins
Jack, 59

Hawshaw
Henry, 73
Jim, 73
Tom, 73

Hendon
Aquila, 96
Arthur, 59
Dave, 73
Dela, 73
Sanford, 73, 96

Hendrick
Anna A., 78

Hendrix
Robert, 225

Henley
E. W., 65
Earnest W., 59

Hensley
Guy, 59
Milton, 58

Hewitt
Katie, 190
Leslie, 58

Hicks
Bert, 58

Hill
Augustus Henry, 169
Charles, 170, 212
Dora Ramsey, 211
Earl, 170
Emma, 181
Estella, 170
F. A., 170
Frank, 58, 63, 212, 213
Fred, 170, 171
Fred A., 169
Pauline, 170
William, 170
Wilmer, 58

Hillis
Bill, 160, 164

Hodges
Chester, 60
Wilson, 60

Holliman
Jake, 179

Hollman
Clifford, 51
Jacob M. "Jake", 59
Jake, 51, 57

Holt
A., 205
Cecil, 162
Doward, 159
Eter, 205
Jimmy, 159
John, 73
John W., 205
Lula, 73, 162
M. A., 205
Neely, 73

Samuel, 225

Hood, 33
John Bell, 24

Hopkins
John, 60

Hornbuckle, 211, 212

Houston
Ellie, 197

Howell
Terry, 155

Hughes
Mary Rickard, 115

Hunt
Edsel, 225
Roy and Edsel, 221
Walker, 117

Hutchins, 134

Hyde
Lando, 60

I

Ingram
Thomas B., 51, 60

J

Jackson
Andrew, 4, 9, 38, 77
Frank, 196
Hattie Mae, 225
James, 4, 38
Oscar, 122

James
Arthur, 60
Edward N., 190

M

P

Reeder
Una White, 211

Reynolds
Clay, 140, 141
Thomas, 60
Thomas H., 140
Will, 60

Richard
Collins, 123

Richardson
Abner, 211
Aubrey, 212
B. F., 211
Brandon, 59
Mary, 211
William McDonald, 84

Rickard
Becky, 102
David, 60
Dorothy (Holland), 102
Dusty, 102, 173
Emmett, 60
F. A. (or Fred), 59
Frank, 73, 90, 101, 165
Fred, 60
Herschel, 223
Hilma Dean, 102
Homer, 101, 102, 153, 171
Homer and Sexter Butler, 102
Hunter, 59, 64, 101
James, 102, 153
James "Dusty", 102
James and Mary Frances
  Redding, 101
Jim, 102
Mary, 73

Mary Frances Redding, 102
Nathan, 102, 153, 175
Nathan Homer, 115
Oscar, 59
Price, 59
Rome, 59, 63, 213
Thomas, 102, 153
Timothy, 59
Will, 73

Rickenbacker
Eddie, 81

Riddell
James William, 221

Riley
Ludie, 205
Thisbe Koonce, 192

Risner
Dick, 59
John, 59
Reed, 59

Roach, 59

Robbins, 83
O. A., 78

Robert
Dendy, 60
Jimmy, 60
Logan, 60

Roberts
Gladys Redding, 211
John, 60
Shaler S., Sr., 51, 61

Robinett
Laura Ann, 150

Robinson
Carol, 81

Tucker
Paul, 130
Pink, 81
Sally, 211
Web, 152, 163
Turnbull
D. B., 51, 60
D. H., 51, 61
Turner, 61

U

Uncle Champ, 12, 18, 20
Uncle Mose, 108

V

Veid
J. J., 90, 140
Vessell
Dent, 61
Floyd E., 60
Hal, 211
Luther, 60
Valton, 212

W

Walters
Red, 163
Waldrop, 61
A. B., 205
M. J., 205
Walker
Frank, 61
Wallace
M. B., 164

Ward
Edward, 38
Ware
William, 61
Warner
Bobby, 81
Washington
George, 64
Waters
Bettie, 193
Watson
Albert, 61
Bob, 160
C. M., 196
Freddie, 211
Lorene, 147
Robert, 61
W. A., 146
W. E., 211
W. G., 205
Willodean, 212
Wayne
Mad Anthony, 64
Weakley
Samuel, 17
Weeden
Elizabeth, 220
Howard, 20, 22, 111
Jesse, 16
Jessie Earthman, 9, 220
John and Jessie, 104, 223
John D., 9, 104, 220, 223, 224
John D. and Jesse, 105
John D.,Sr., 111
John Downing, 219
Martha Patton, 9

REFERENCES BOOKS AND PUBLISHED DOCUMENTS:

Chaudacoff, Howard P., "The Evolution of Urban Society" (Prentice Hall, New Jersey, 1975).

Kelso, Mrs. Thurman "A History of The First Presbyterian Church, Florence, Alabama" (1968)

UNPUBLISHED PAPERS AND PRIVATE COLLECTIONS;

Dendy, Eva, "East Florence", April 17, 1977. Irons Orlan, early newspaper collection.

Johnson, Franklin Pierce Papers (in possession of author).

Lewis, Oscar *D.,* private papers and articles that have appeared in the Florence Times and Florence Herald over a period of twenty years.

Merrill, Susan "East Florence Business District", May 1976.

Sheridan, Richard C., private papers.

Staggs, L. D. Jr., private papers, newspaper clippings and early photographs.

Watts, Charles Wilder, private papers

Williford, Theo., Sr., early newspaper collection.

Wright, Milly, private papers.

INTERVIEWS:

Hall James F. Sr., March 19, 1971.

McDonald, Ervin, April 6, 1983.

Plott, Irma Matthews, September 18, 1988.

Published by

Bluewater Publications is a multi-faceted publishing company capable of meeting all of your reading and publishing needs. Our two-fold aim is to:

1) Provide the market with educationally enlightening and inspiring research and reading materials and to

2) Make the opportunity of being published available to any author and or researcher who so desires to become published.

We are passionate about preserving history; whether it is through the re-publishing of an out-of-print classic or by publishing the research of historians and genealogists, Bluewater Publications is the publisher you need.

To learn more about the Dr. William Lindsey McDonald or for information about how you can be published through Bluewater Publications, please visit:

www.BluewaterPublications.com

Confidently Preserving Our Past,
Bluewater Publications.com
Formerly Known as Heart of Dixie Publishing

www.ingramcontent.com/pod-product-compliance
Lightning Source LLC
Chambersburg PA
CBHW080457110426
42742CB00017B/2919

9780971994638